A SPACE SYNTAX ANALYSIS OF ARROYO HONDO PUEBLO

ARROYO HONDO ARCHAEOLOGICAL SERIES

James F. Brooks
General Editor

The Contemporary Ecology of Arroyo Hondo, New Mexico
N. Edmund Kelley

Prehistoric Pueblo Settlement Patterns:
The Arroyo Hondo, New Mexico, Site Survey
D. Bruce Dickson, Jr.

Pueblo Populations and Society:
The Arroyo Hondo Skeletal and Mortuary Remains
Ann M. Palkovich

The Past Climate of Arroyo Hondo, New Mexico, Reconstructed from Tree Rings
Martin R. Rose, Jeffrey S. Dean, and William J. Robinson

The Faunal Remains from Arroyo Hondo, New Mexico:
A Study in Short-Term Subsistence Change
Richard W. Lang and Arthur H. Harris

The Architecture of Arroyo Hondo Pueblo, New Mexico
Winifred Creamer

The Pottery from Arroyo Hondo, New Mexico:
Tribalization and Trade in the Northern Rio Grande
Judith A. Habicht-Mauche

A Space Syntax Analysis of Arroyo Hondo Pueblo, New Mexico:
Community Formation in the Northern Rio Grande
Jason S. Shapiro

A SPACE SYNTAX ANALYSIS OF ARROYO HONDO PUEBLO, NEW MEXICO

COMMUNITY FORMATION IN THE NORTHERN RIO GRANDE

Jason S. Shapiro

SCHOOL OF AMERICAN RESEARCH PRESS
SANTA FE, NEW MEXICO

SCHOOL OF AMERICAN RESEARCH PRESS
Post Office Box 2188
Santa Fe, New Mexico 87504-2188
www.press.sarweb.org

Acting Director: Catherine Cocks
Manuscript Editor: Jane Kepp
Design and Production: Cynthia Dyer
Proofreader: Kate Talbot
Indexer: Catherine Fox
Printer: Thomson Shore, Inc.

Library of Congress Cataloging-in-Publication Data

Shapiro, Jason S.
  A space syntax analysis of Arroyo Hondo Pueblo, New Mexico: community
formation in the northern Rio Grande/Jason S. Shapiro.
      p. cm. — (Arroyo Hondo archaeological series)
  Includes bibliographical references and index.
  ISBN 1-930618-59-X (pa : alk. paper)
  1. Arroyo Hondo Site (N.M.). 2. Pueblo Indians—Antiquities. 3. Pueblo
architecture—New Mexico. 4. Ethnoarchaeology—New Mexico. 5. Environmental
archaeology—New Mexico. 6. Rio Grande Valley—Antiquities. I. Title. II. Series.

E99.P9S525 2005
978.9'53--dc22

                                                          2005013479

Dedicated to Celia

Cover credit: Excavations at Arroyo Hondo Pueblo, 1970s © School of
American Research.

CONTENTS

FIGURES

vii

TABLES

FOREWORD

During the early years of the fourteenth century C.E., a major new settlement arose at the base of the Sangre de Cristo Mountains, five miles southeast of what was later to become Santa Fe, New Mexico (fig. 2.1). This community, named Arroyo Hondo Pueblo by archaeologists, grew rapidly from a few residences to nearly a thousand rooms and perhaps as many occupants by the year 1330. Prior to this time, all the settlements in the northern Rio Grande Valley were much smaller, closer to one hundred rooms, so this new, fast-growing settlement was a massive boom town compared with earlier villages. Although abandoned after only about 125 years, Arroyo Hondo Pueblo was one of the forerunners and prototypes of the large pueblos that the Spanish encountered when they arrived two centuries later.

In 1970, I initiated a major archaeological research project at Arroyo Hondo Pueblo. This work had three central objectives: to use the most current and comprehensive techniques to expand our understanding of prehistoric northern Rio Grande Pueblo culture, to explore the growth and dynamics of a large Pueblo IV settlement, and to use Arroyo Hondo Pueblo, along with comparative ethnographic analysis, to examine the cross-cultural implications of rapid population growth and cultural and environmental change (Schwartz 1971).

Over the past three decades, the fieldwork at Arroyo Hondo Pueblo yielded fundamental new information about fourteenth-century life in the northern Rio Grande Valley. Because the site was built and abandoned in a relatively short period of time, and because no large, later prehistoric or historic pueblo was constructed above it, the full architectural layout and construction sequence of the pueblo, with all their changes over time, are clearly visible. Five seasons of excavation at Arroyo Hondo and almost two decades of analysis, writing, and publication have provided an extraordinary opportunity to understand the life of this community and learn about the cultural region of which it was a part. The present volume, the ninth in the Arroyo Hondo monograph series, examines the architecture from the perspective of the space syntax methodology.

HISTORY OF THE ARROYO HONDO PROJECT

Research at Arroyo Hondo began in 1970 with a survey and test excavations designed to determine the nature of the site. Based on this and later work, the National Science Foundation provided funds to support the field phase of the project (grants GS-28001 and GS 42181). Between 1971 and 1974, we carried out a systematic program of excavation focusing on room and roomblock architecture, site organization and growth, residential configuration, and plaza and kiva design and use. In addition, we conducted a regional archaeological survey and an extensive ecological analysis.

During the years of excavation, we published interim results in three preliminary reports (Schwartz 1971, 1972; Schwartz and Lang 1973). In 1974, upon completion of the fieldwork, we made a film—*The Rio Grande's Pueblo Past*—with support from the National Geographic Society and showed it to their membership at Constitution Hall in Washington, D.C. It illustrated the history of the project and presented some initial conclusions. After completing several years of analysis, I also published a preliminary synthesis of the work (Schwartz 1981).

Since the original conception of the Arroyo Hondo project, more than thirty years have passed. Over that time, we published a major series of monographs. In addition, I received an important grant from the National Endowment for the Humanities to create a permanent repository and laboratory to house the Arroyo Hondo Pueblo excavated material, field notes, and photographs at the School of American Research (SAR). This facility and an SAR summer fellowship supporting research on the collections make it possible for a new generation of scholars to use the collection to ask new questions about the site and reexamine the original conclusions.

The pursuit of large, long-term archaeological projects, like that at Arroyo Hondo, presents several challenges. It requires a persistence of vision and responsibility to the project extending beyond the fieldwork phase. Many such projects bog down or end only half way to meeting their intended objective for lack of personnel continuity; they falter in the analysis of the vast amounts of varied data that result from the excavation; or they wane during the writing, editing, and publication of manuscripts. Furthermore, those involved in large, long-running site projects must be prepared to refine and elaborate their original questions as they incorporate the results of analysis and current archeological thinking.

ARCHAEOLOGICAL BACKGROUND

For centuries, settlements in the northern Rio Grande Valley lagged significantly behind the rest of the ancestral Pueblo world in population size and cultural complexity. Although people had lived in the region for thousands of years, the first farming villages did not appear until about 600 C.E. Over the next three centuries, Rio Grande settlers lived in small, scattered farmsteads, surviving on a combination of foraging and horticulture. They resided in circular pit houses or aboveground adobe rooms and moved seasonally to take advantage of the widest variety of resources. During this time, the region remained marginal to the more highly developed Chaco and Four Corners Pueblo areas.

In the middle of the 1200s, population in the northern Rio Grande Valley began increasing, and the first medium-sized villages appeared—settlements with a dozen to 150 rooms, some containing two or more sets of roomblocks facing into a plaza with a kiva. Despite their larger size, these villages continued to be built in the prevailing local architectural style, and their inhabitants used locally made pottery.

The late thirteenth century also saw the beginnings of a transition in settlement configuration to large towns scattered throughout the Southwest. With some five hundred to one thousand rooms, these settlements were far bigger than earlier communities. Point of Pines and Grasshopper in central Arizona, Awatovi in the Hopi country of northern Arizona, Casa Grandes in northern Mexico, and others in the Zuni country south of Gallup exemplify the trend. Arroyo Hondo Pueblo was one of the early large towns built in the northern Rio Grande

Valley, so we expected our excavation of the site to yield clues to the reasons behind this shift from smaller villages to major towns.

ARROYO HONDO PUEBLO

Around 1300 C.E., a few families found a location for a new settlement that offered a good building site, a free-flowing spring, well-watered soil in an adjacent canyon, and easy access to a number of ecological zones containing a wide range of plants and animals. Taking advantage of these special qualities, the founding settlers of Arroyo Hondo Pueblo built an alignment of masonry rooms along the edge of a 125-foot gorge.

From the start, agriculture played an important part in the pueblo's economy. Land in the bottom of the Arroyo Hondo could support floodwater farming, and the surrounding higher terrain could be dry farmed. The settlers probably planted their first fields of corn, beans, and squash in the arroyo and supplemented their harvests by gathering seasonally available wild greens, seeds, and nuts from a territory of about eight square miles. Among the more than ninety species of animals available to the hunters of Arroyo Hondo, deer provided a major source of their protein; rabbits, antelope, and bison were also significant items in the diet.

Residents of Arroyo Hondo traded actively with other communities in the region, probably exchanging food and locally made ceramics. They also obtained resources from more distant areas: painted turtles from villages to the south along the Rio Grande, shells indirectly from the Pacific coast and Gulf of California, and live macaws from what is now northern Mexico.

The pueblo grew rapidly during its first two or three decades, ultimately expanding to one thousand rooms in twenty-four roomblocks of one- and two-story apartments, clustered around ten plazas (fig. 2.2). During the late 1330s, a significant drop in annual precipitation may have led to inferior harvests and declining availability of wild plants and animals, making it difficult for the residents of such a large community to feed themselves. Even without a drought, the mere presence of so many people depleted local resources. Over the years, firewood became increasingly difficult to obtain, and other resources previously taken for granted may have been nearing exhaustion. Skeletal remains suggest that the people of Arroyo Hondo suffered from food shortages.

Malnutrition—especially iron deficiency—complicated by infectious diseases resulted in the death of more than half of all children under the age of five, and the average life expectancy was miserably low (Palkovich 1980).

Consistent food shortages and the scarcity of firewood posed serious problems sparking a range of social complications. The founding residents of Arroyo Hondo had come from much smaller communities, where the means for resolving conflicts were well established. At Arroyo Hondo, however, as the settlement grew to some two or three hundred families, new social mechanisms may have become necessary to allocate land and settle disputes.

Soon after 1335, the town's population shrank dramatically. As rooms in the pueblo fell into disuse, some became trash dumps and others filled with wind-blown dirt after people removed their roof timbers to use as firewood, a practice that caused the roofs to collapse. The reasons for the town's abandonment are not entirely clear, but environmental change was certainly one of them. By 1345, Arroyo Hondo was virtually or more likely completely abandoned. For the next thirty years, the derelict pueblo was vacant or, at most, used only by a small remnant or seasonal population. This abandonment marked the end of the Component I occupation.

Sometime during the 1370s, precipitation increased and a second phase of settlement began. The "Component II" pueblo, built on top of the ruins of the earlier town, was smaller than the first occupation but very like it in architecture and layout. The new villagers, who may have been descendants of the original settlers, again probably saw the old location, with a spring in the arroyo and good farmland, as a superior location to settle. At its peak, this later village contained only two hundred rooms organized in nine roomblocks around three plazas (fig. 2.2). The renewed growth was short-lived, however. Soon after 1410, drought again began devastating the region. Then a catastrophic fire destroyed a significant part of the settlement. Within a few years, the drought reached a severity unprecedented in the history of the pueblo—the lowest annual precipitation in a thousand years, according to the local tree-ring record. With this last adversity, the second and final occupation of Arroyo Hondo Pueblo ended.

Before the Spaniards arrived in the Rio Grande Valley and filled much of the land then unoccupied by Native Americans, Pueblo people moved their villages frequently. Whether the reasons were environmental, social, or a combination of the two, moving and re-building villages—even very large settlements—was a common prac-tice (Lekson 1990). The cycles of construction and abandonment at Arroyo Hondo exemplify just how rapidly these large villages could be built and how swiftly they could become vacant.

THE ARROYO HONDO PUBLICATION SERIES

Arroyo Hondo was a large and complicated project. In my origi-nal research design, I decided to involve a number of scholars with spe-cialized backgrounds and knowledge in various aspects of the project. I intended each of these researchers to follow his or her particular part of the project from the fieldwork to analysis and to write a published report on his or her findings. With this kind of continuity, I believed, all the staff could become familiar with the evolution of the research results, concentrate on an area of specialization related to the project, build expertise over the life of the project, and, as members of an ongo-ing team, stay conversant with the results of the other aspects of the project. My objective was to produce in this way a series of publica-tions containing a detailed presentation of data and also allow these individual researchers to add important new ideas to our understand-ing of Southwestern prehistory.

The multivolume Arroyo Hondo publication series received par-tial support from another National Science Foundation grant (BNS 76-83501). As the analysis progressed and the potential contribution of various topics to the overall project became clear, the composition of the publication series changed somewhat. Some studies originally planned as full volumes, such as the pollen analysis and the description of stone artifacts, developed into shorter reports or appendixes. Other work planned for shorter reports ultimately became so important that we published them as major monographs, such as the work on dendroclimatology.

Completing a publication series of this sort involves a number of challenges. These include the amount of time a researcher-author can spend on the work, the individual's persistence and motivation, the degree to which the project competes with the author's other life goals and responsibilities, differences in the time taken to complete various volumes and thus differences in the availability of results to the other authors, differences in research and writing ability, and the continual need to obtain new funding to support ongoing analysis and publication. No project of this kind can avoid these and similar problems, and, unfortunately, it is not possible to predict or control them in the initial stages of work or as the work progresses.

The plan of moving from fieldwork to manuscripts succeeded exceptionally well for the first six volumes in the series, all of which were written by scholars who had joined the project early in the fieldwork stage. Some, advanced graduate students, I invited to use the Arroyo Hondo material for a thesis (Kelley [1980] examined the pueblo's ecology) or for dissertations (Dickson [1979] wrote up the regional site survey; Palkovich [1980] analyzed the skeletal and mortuary remains; Wetterstrom [1986] discussed archaeobotany). Others were members of the School of American Research's archaeological staff, often working with outside experts (Lang and Harris [1984] performed the faunal analysis), or they were consultants asked to analyze some aspect of the data (Rose, Dean, and Robinson [1981] explored the dendroclimatology).

Soon after we completed the excavations at Arroyo Hondo, I asked two key members of the field project to initiate the seventh and eighth monographs in the series, covering ceramics and architecture. Richard W. Lang undertook a comprehensive description and seriation of the ceramics, and John D. Beal wrote an initial manuscript on architecture. However, Lang and Beal moved on to other work before finishing their final manuscripts. Taking up the ceramics volume, Judith A. Habicht-Mauche (1993) went beyond description to consider the development of the regional social system of which Arroyo Hondo was a part. Winifred Creamer (1993) developed further Beal's architecture manuscript by examining the growth, organization, and decline of the Arroyo Hondo community. In addition to the monographs, shorter reports have been published on regional metric comparisons of the skeletal collection (Mackey 1980); pollen studies (Bohrer 1986); artifacts of wood (Lang 1986); ceramic artifacts (Thibodeau 1993); bone artifacts (Beach and Causey [1984]); shell artifacts (Venn 1984); hide, fur, and feathers (Lang 1984); lithics (Phagan 1993); and stratigraphic ceramic samples (Lang 1993).

As this publication record indicates, the use of numerous skilled individuals as analysts and authors was advantageous in spite of delays, changes in authors, and the additional expense of restarting writing projects left incomplete. Research on small sites may yield faster returns, but the amount of data and the depth of the interpretation that can emerge from work at larger sites like Arroyo Hondo, if continued to completion, justify the extended effort. As I look back over the contents of the published volumes, I feel that they have all accomplished our original objectives and added significantly to our understanding of both Arroyo Hondo and Southwestern prehistory.

With the publication of the first eight volumes in the Arroyo Hondo series, the basic description and consideration of the excavated and related materials are complete. As a result, we enter a new direction in our deliberations about Arroyo Hondo and the contribution it can make to Southwestern archaeology. The current volume in the series is the first to embark upon this second phase. While the original monographs and reports grew directly out of the field project, in this monograph Jason Shapiro examines the Arroyo Hondo excavation records and collections and asks new questions from a new perspective. It is my hope that we will see future research and publication of this kind, reexamining material from the site with new techniques and new inquiries.

A SPACE SYNTAX ANALYSIS OF ARROYO HONDO PUEBLO

Shapiro for the first time applies the technique of space syntax, a relatively new methodology initiated outside of archaeology, to architectural changes at Arroyo Hondo Pueblo and other sites in the northern Rio Grande. He poses several questions about the relationship between changes in architecture and shifts in social organization in the social context of the period 1200 to 1600 C.E. In doing this, he demonstrates that an in-depth application of space syntax to this archaeological context can shed new light on old questions.

Showing a clear command of space syntax theory and methods, Dr. Shapiro does a thorough job of illustrating the benefits of applying this rather technical approach to archaeology. By linking the social and the spatial, he successfully shows the role of architecture in shaping and being shaped by human behavior. Using this approach on the Arroyo Hondo site, he explores the changing organization of public and domestic space and the increasing control of interior space by what appear to be nuclear families. In analyzing the organization of space, Shapiro illuminates the distinctive rules that "control the manner in which people segregate and connect space…and explain how space was both arranged and correlated with the social and political behavior that characterized" (pp. 6, 7) Arroyo Hondo Pueblo.

Douglas W. Schwartz

PREFACE

This study developed from two observations I made—though neither of them was original to me—in the mid-1990s while planning the dissertation upon which this book is based. The first was that current political, economic, and social realities had made it more difficult for archaeologists to dig new holes in the ground. I don't mean that no one excavates anymore, but only that the era of large-scale, multiyear, massively funded projects is probably past, and a great deal of future "digging" will be among the curated collections maintained by museums and universities.

The second observation was that the extraordinary effort that had been devoted to describing, classifying, and interpreting artifacts such as pottery and stone tools had not been applied to the largest and most impressive class of archaeologically recorded material, namely, architecture. It is not that archaeologists have ignored architecture, but much of what they have published involves detailed descriptive treatments that sometimes fail to connect buildings with their builders in meaningful ways. These observations suggested then and now that a great deal of work is still to be done in the Southwest in which new analytical techniques can be applied to the "treasures" waiting to be discovered in archives, storage boxes, and filing cabinets.

For their help in exploring some of those treasures, I am pleased to thank the following people. Special gratitude goes to the late James Hatch, my dissertation advisor and the chairman of my dissertation committee at the Pennsylvania State University, whose help, encouragement, and fine editorial contributions were indispensable to the completion of the original study on which this book is based. In addition, recognition must be given to the other members of my dissertation committee, Sidney Cohn, Winifred Creámer, George Milner, and David Webster, all of whom supported, contributed to, and encouraged me in the completion of this work.

A great deal of gratitude is extended to Douglas Schwartz, former president of the School of American Research in Santa Fe, New Mexico, as well as to the current administration and staff of SAR for their generosity and willingness to provide unlimited access to the Arroyo Hondo Pueblo collection and to allow me to use and reproduce a variety of documentary materials. Special appreciation goes to James Brooks, director of the SAR Press, and Catherine Cocks, senior editor of the press, for their continuing patience, interest in, and support of what at times appeared to be a languishing project.

Appreciation is also given to Bruce Huckell, Brenda Dorr, and the staff at the Maxwell Museum of Anthropology in Albuquerque, New Mexico, for their generous assistance, cooperation, and support in providing access to the Tijeras Pueblo collections and for allowing me to reproduce any number of documents and maps. Thanks also to David Hurst Thomas ans Lori Peterson of the American Museum of Natural History.

Particular recognition must be given to Bill Hillier, Julienne Hanson, and their colleagues at the Bartlett School in London, who formulated the relevant concepts on which this study is based and who graciously allowed me to use the analytical software they developed. It is no overstatement to say that without Hillier and Hanson, this book would never have been written.

Although myriad people provided useful suggestions in connection with this project, several offered invaluable comments, ideas, or editorial inputs that are incorporated in some fashion in the final product. These persons include David Wilcox, Wendy Bustard, Laurel Cooper, Catherine Cameron, and, in particular, Linda Cordell. Absent Linda's insightful questions, comments, and support, I am not sure that this book would ever have been published. Finally, I offer my deepest appreciation to Jane Kepp, my editor, whose hard work helped turn a reasonable manuscript into something worthy of publication.

Thanks to the assistance of all these people, this book is much better than it otherwise would have been. Any errors of omission or commission are my own, and I take full responsibility for them.

A SPACE SYNTAX ANALYSIS OF ARROYO HONDO PUEBLO

1
Introduction

Societies are always spatial, and spaces are always social.
—*Thomas A. Markus,* Buildings and Power

In this book I examine architectural changes among the ancestral Pueblo (or "Anasazi") inhabitants of Arroyo Hondo Pueblo and other fourteenth- and fifteenth-century settlements in what is now the northern Rio Grande Valley of New Mexico. I develop the idea of spatial organization as an embodiment of social organization, employing "space" as an artifact that archaeologists might study more intensively than they generally have in the past. I believe built space must be treated as one of many independent variables in the study of culture. It may be the case that, as the archaeologist Richard Wilshusen (1989: 831) expressed it, "the origin of Anasazi architectural changes...is to be found in changes in social or economic organization," but I want to begin with architectural remains and work backward in order to reveal something about social organization.

The Arroyo Hondo project, which generated the data I use in this book, began in 1970 and continued over nearly ten years under the

3

direction of Douglas W. Schwartz and the School of American Research in Santa Fe, New Mexico (Schwartz 1971, 1972; Schwartz and Lang 1973). As an integral part of the study, Schwartz and his team systematically excavated approximately 150 rooms representing almost all of the pueblo's 24 roomblocks. Researchers associated with the project analyzed the rooms, roomblocks, and adjacent plaza areas from a variety of perspectives, producing information about architectural features, settlement organization and growth, residential configurations, and the nature and uses of plazas. I cite their work frequently throughout this book.

It became clear to me early on that innovations in the way in which architectural space was arranged, particularly in the relative ease with which residents could gain access to different kinds of spaces such as living rooms and storage rooms, could be discerned from Arroyo Hondo's archaeological record. That spatial arrangements changed over time—from one of the site's two major components of occupation to the other—without a corresponding change in material culture was a second and somewhat unexpected conclusion. Ultimately, the study suggests that people change the manner in which they organize their built spaces in order to facilitate or inhibit social encounters. Whether such encounters are encouraged or discouraged at any particular time reflects the changing nature of the society being studied in terms of its internal (in this case, intrapueblo) and external social relationships.

THE SOCIAL AND THE SPATIAL

The epigraph from Thomas Markus encapsulates the theme of this study, which is that the ways in which people structure their social relations relate to the ways in which they organize their spaces (Gutman 1972). In what follows, I navigate the interface between archaeology, a discipline that seeks to recover social information from material remains, and architecture, a discipline that designs structures that embody social information (Rapoport 1990:185–239). When considering the connections between archaeology and architecture, Amos Rapoport (1980:288) observed that "any artifact can be seen as the result of a series of choices among various alternatives. The design process, that is, the shaping of any kind of environment, can also be seen as a series of choices made from a set of alternatives. How these choices are made, what is included or excluded, and how various elements are ranked in terms of high or low value, leads to specific environments." A slightly different view was expressed by David Saile (1977:159), who wrote that "archaeology and architecture correspond in their concern with understanding the ways in which people, people-adapted 'things' (including architecture) and the external natural environment are related and how and why those relationships change over time.... A key factor which distinguishes the two disciplines, however, is the concern of architecture with spatial aspects of the built environment."

Since the late nineteenth century, anthropologists and archaeologists have sought to investigate the congruence between social structures and built structures. Lewis Henry Morgan (1881), Victor Mindeleff (1891), and Emil Durkheim (1964 [1893]) all examined the ways in which behavior and built forms accommodate and reinforce each other, and they all argued that the social order is not only reflected but actually reproduced in the spatial ordering of a society (Lawrence and Low 1990:456). Every culture creates its own distinct architecture, but how these forms differ in time and space is a much easier question to answer than *why* they differ.

The orientation with which one approaches the relationship between a society and its built environment depends in some measure on whether one is trained in the design professions or the social and behavioral sciences. People trained in the former tend to focus on tangible forms, structures, and materials; those trained in the latter tend to focus on intangible ideational and cultural concepts. Overarching theoretical perspectives that might link the two groups have never been in short supply, but the use of specialized jargon and the proliferation of theoretical perspectives within each group have acted to separate practitioners rather than help develop a unified theory of "buildings and behavior" (Horgan 1995). Some efforts at a synthesis continue to be made (e.g., Markus 1972; Kent 1990; Blanton 1994), but the fundamental point of separation among the multiplicity of approaches seems to be between those that are largely descriptive, empirical, and intuitive and those that are theoretical, analytic, and predictive. Proponents of most theories seem to recognize correlations between built forms and social relationships (Pearson and Richards 1994), but they differ in their explanations of the nature, strength, and meaning of those correlations.

Among the authors who have attempted to synthesize ideas about architecture and behavior, Denise Lawrence and Setha Low, in their essay "The Built Environment and Spatial Form" (1990), published one of the most comprehensive compilations of architectural, anthropological, and psychological theories. Despite its ambitiousness, this survey of epistemological and ontological orientations ultimately failed to offer any means of assessing the explanatory value of the plethora of theories. The authors acknowledged that theories of social production—those that "focus on the social, political, and economic forces that produce the built environment" together with "the impact of the socially produced built environment on social action"—are the most promising areas for anthropological inquiry (Lawrence and Low 1990:482). Their study, however, was more a compendium of what has been considered than it was the basis for a research design.

Nold Egenter, on the other hand, championed the development of what he called "architectural anthropology" (1992b:12), which "wants to look anthropologically at architecture and, in reverse, intends to carry out research into anthropology from the point of view of architecture" (1992a:22–23). He argued for a systematic approach to the study of architecture that was scientific in its orientation and cross-disciplinary in its scope, in some respects echoing the tenets proposed by practitioners of the New Archaeology three decades earlier. Irrespective of whether Egenter provided an outline for a new approach to architectural theory or merely restated environment-behavior themes originally investigated by Rapoport (1980, 1990) and others, he set forth the kind of interdisciplinary framework I used to structure the present study.

My basic assumption is that spatial use patterns are not the results of unconscious decisions but arise from purposeful responses to architectural needs that are consonant with environmental, demographic, and behavioral factors (Hillier and Hanson 1984; Horne 1994). By the same token, built forms influence residential behavioral patterns. An analysis of prehistoric pueblos reveals the existence of an underlying set of rules that explain how space was both arranged and correlated with the social and political behavior that characterized those societies. My ultimate conclusion is that it is possible to study the process of organizational change by analyzing the process of architectural change. The unifying logic that underlies spatial and social organization is discoverable through a quantitative approach developed by two British architects, Bill Hillier and Julienne Hanson, that is called *space syntax analysis.*

6

SPACE SYNTAX AND ARCHITECTURE AS ARTIFACT

In *The Social Logic of Space* (Hillier and Hanson 1984) and numerous other publications (Hanson 1998; Hillier, Leaman, et al. 1976; Hillier 1985, 1989, 1996; Hillier, Hanson, and Graham 1987; Hillier, Hanson, and Peponis 1987), the authors describe a philosophy that explains how social groups configure their spaces to satisfy fundamental social needs. They explain a set of techniques that reduce the spatial configurations of buildings and settlements to geometric networks described by series of numbers. Ultimately, the concept involves quantifying the multiple relationships among all the spaces in a system (Hillier, Hanson, and Graham 1987; Hillier 1996). A cornerstone of the theory is an assumption that the configuration of any network of built spaces is the spatial expression of the social relations of the group responsible for creating the network. The underlying logic of any built environment then becomes the arrangement of space, rather than the creation of buildings. In more concrete terms, "the primary purpose of a barn is not the edifice but the ordered spaces that the building provides for the storage of tools, resources and livestock. If the ordering of space determines modes of social interaction, then buildings have sociological meaning" (Ferguson 1993:36).

Hillier and Hanson conceive of architecture (or the process of creating a built environment) as one of several manifestations of an underlying cultural process. The domain of architecture is not separate from the domains of economics, politics, and social organization but relates to each cultural element as it, in turn, relates to every other element according to underlying structural principles (see, e.g., Hodder 1990: 56). Hillier's writings have always stressed that space is a cultural artifact whose visible forms are arranged according to fundamental cultural paradigms that organize and direct social processes (Hillier 1996:91–93). All people with "normal vision" can visually experience space, or see it in three-dimensional terms, but the way in which any space is interpreted depends upon individual and culturally mediated views.

Operationally, space syntax analysis is based on the assumption that rules exist that control the manner in which people segregate and connect space. It rests on a conception of the built environment that considers spaces in terms of their boundaries (i.e., whether they are open or closed) and relationships (i.e., whether they are contiguous or discontiguous). Physical structures are reduced to simplified networks of

7

nodes (spaces) and *linkages* (doors, corridors, roads) that can be analyzed in terms of people's potential ease of movement through the network and, ultimately, the potential for social interaction to take place in the structures.

Architectural remains constitute some of the best examples of cultural activity found in the archaeological record. They reflect purposeful patterns that can be described in terms of sets of relationships among built forms that result from recurrent human behaviors. Ancestral Pueblo architecture in the northern Rio Grande has been characterized as irregular arrangements of regular forms in sequences that responded to critical needs such as shelter, defense, and spiritual well-being (Hieb 1992; Swentzell 1992; Wilcox and Haas 1994), but there is also a coherence in those arrangements that is not readily apparent. In its simplest terms, architecture impresses a social "fingerprint" upon the landscape, a behavioral code that can be read and interpreted. I hope to demonstrate that space syntax analysis is one way to "read" those fingerprints, and the particular fingerprint to which I have applied the methodology is Arroyo Hondo Pueblo.

2

Archaeology, the Built Environment, and Arroyo Hondo Pueblo

What we know of "space" in general is of little help in assisting
us to grasp it as an actual entity.
—*Lazlo Moholy-Nagy, "Space, Space-Time, and the Photographer"*

Every human culture manipulates the space it occupies. Such manipulations vary from simple arrangements such as the brush shelters constructed by the !Kung of southern Africa (Draper 1973) to the complex constructions erected by contemporary urban societies. The ways in which different societies arrange space to create unique built environments and the ways in which those environments correspond to social forms within the societies are unresolved but much-debated issues among both architects and anthropologists. One common theme is that architectural forms organize space for social purposes, with the corollary that cultural information resides in the physical forms of buildings and settlements in the same way it can reside in ceramic or lithic artifacts (Hillier and Hanson 1987). It is not difficult to recover such information from contemporary or historical structures in which use functions and design assumptions may be observed, but when archaeologists examine

9

prehistoric settlements, for which no contemporaneous written documentation exists, their principal clues to past spatial behavior are the surviving architectural elements themselves.

Although in this study I test the application of space syntax analysis to prehistoric architecture, my project is really no different from that of analyzing any other type of artifact. Architecture, like other material constructs, can be manipulated to convey information (Habicht-Mauche 1993, 1995; Pearson and Richards 1994; Moore 1996; Nelson 1996). As with pottery or stone tools, one endeavors to identify certain traits, classify them in some meaningful way, observe how they changed over time, and discover the selective forces that influenced the changes (Shafer 1995). In this vein, a number of other researchers have looked at architectural technology as a source of social and cultural information (Reynolds 1981; Stark, Clark, and Elson 1995).

In the present study, I am less concerned with the actual technology of building than with resultant networks of constructed spaces. Although more familiar artifactual analyses involving lithic (Nelson 1996) and ceramic (Crown 1994; Mills and Crown 1995) forms and designs have often focused on production, distribution, and consumption, they fit within the larger issues of cultural development and change, which can encompass architecture. For example, one hypothesis suggests that decorative designs on ceramics serve as social markers that can be "read" to distinguish social boundaries between ethnic or other groups (Habicht-Mauche 1993, 1995). These "stylistic boundaries" may define households, villages, or regions, but whatever the organizational scale, they operate to distinguish groups—the "us" from the "them"—and they implicitly incorporate spatial components ("we live here and our pottery looks like this; they live over there and their pottery looks like that").

Other researchers have examined the ways in which social and spatial elements interact and have come tantalizingly close to meshing them in a unified conceptual framework. For example, Kelley Hays-Gilpin recognized the connection among visual arts, social differentiation, and spatial aggregation (Hays 1993), though she proposed no mechanism to connect them. J. J. Brody (1991:53–54) compared design elements found in both ancestral Pueblo pottery and architecture in terms of their visual impact and symbolism but inferred no deeper organizational significance from them. Christopher Chippendale (1992) considered the value of applying a variety of grammatical

10

approaches, including space syntax analysis, to the archaeological record but did not take the next step and show how it might actually be done. I believe space syntax analysis can provide the link between the social and the spatial and become an integral part of a comprehensive approach to architectural analysis, analogous to what has been pursued with ceramics. If "style" is a way of doing (Hodder 1990), then space syntax analysis offers a means to understanding ancestral Pueblo society through the "style" of its spatial arrangements. As Erik K. Reed, who investigated the relationships between ancestral Puebloan social structure and settlement forms, put it: "Town plans will surely prove as important as potsherds for this kind of synthesis" (Reed 1956:12).

STUDYING SOCIAL ORGANIZATION
IN THE NORTHERN SOUTHWEST

Cultural evolution among the ancestral Pueblo inhabitants of the northern Southwest encompassed at least 1,200 years of temporal and spatial developments. I am concerned primarily with two cultural periods at the end of the ancestral Pueblo era in the northern Rio Grande Valley (fig. 2.1), the Coalition period (1200–1325 C.E.) and the Classic period (1325–1600), that were characterized by a unique constellation of architectural innovations. The Coalition period witnessed the initial appearance of large settlements with numerous roomblocks constructed around extensive systems of public plazas. These new, plaza-centered pueblos, some of which incorporated hundreds or even thousands of rooms, became the predominant Pueblo architectural form, continuing into the historic period.

Despite more than 100 years of archaeological research, questions about social and political complexity within those settlements are still being debated (compare Bullock 1993; Brandt 1994; Spielmann 1994, Wilcox 1996). Many interpretations of social and political change among the ancestral Pueblos still rely on variations of neo-evolutionary, trait-based schemes (Service 1962; Fried 1967) in which materially defined markers suggest differences in wealth, status, or the exercise of authority. Certain variables have become associated with the existence of social complexity, including differential mortuary treatment, differential house sizes and locations, large settlement size, large population size and high population density, the existence of interregional exchange, and the creation of monumental public architecture. For a

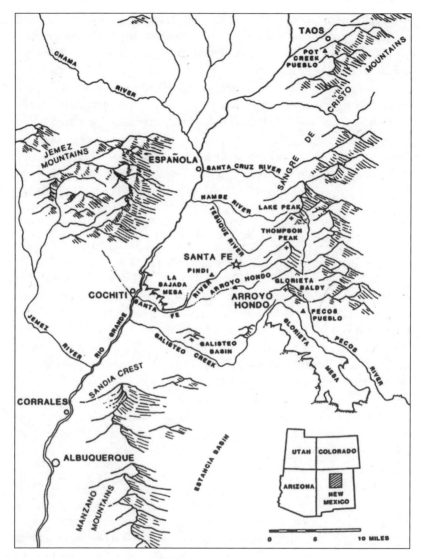

Figure 2.1. Location of Arroyo Hondo Pueblo in the northern Rio Grande region.

number of reasons, these surrogate measures of complexity have failed to provide definite answers to questions about the nature of social and political developments in the northern Southwest during the late pre-historic period. Moreover, they provide no direct linkage between the kind of behavior that has been labeled "sociopolitical complexity" and

12

the many architectural remains found in the region. In some respects, people have been asking the same questions, using variations of the same types of data to answer them, and have obtained many of the same amorphous answers.

Some of the issues inherent in traditional approaches are illustrated by three detailed studies in which researchers considered the social organization of prehistoric pueblos in the northern Rio Grande but reached opposite conclusions about overall levels of complexity. Elizabeth Brandt (1994:14) evaluated social stratification using a framework that relied on six inclusive social characteristics:

1. Hierarchically ranked groups with permanent positions
2. Differential sources of power relative to each group's ranking
3. Differential access to resources
4. Cultural and individual distinctions
5. Ideology providing a rationale for the system
6. Relative degree of inequality of rewards and privileges

Brandt concluded that the late prehistoric pueblos in the Rio Grande were non-egalitarian, multiethnic, hierarchical, centralized communities with multiple levels of decision making; social inequalities were maintained by a system of information control managed through institutions based on secrecy, surveillance, and privacy (Brandt 1994: 20). Although she considered the significance of ritual paraphernalia and the power of religious organizations, she focused less on the symbolic and spiritual nature of ritual practices than on their place in the realpolitik of Pueblo society. She ultimately decided that these communities were stratified as a result of the emergent hierarchies associated with population aggregation, though she suggested no underlying mechanism to explain the evolution of stratification.

Katherine Spielmann (1994), notwithstanding that she examined some of the same data as Brandt, found that the Rio Grande pueblos did not feature social hierarchies or centralized systems for decision making but instead developed more cooperative arrangements, akin to the governing systems identified for the Iroquois and Huron confederacies (Trigger 1990). Using a combination of archaeological and ethnographic sources, Spielmann showed how economic complexity apparently developed without the intercession of social or political hierarchies. She found that the Rio Grande pueblos were characterized by series of temporary alliances that developed for the limited purposes of alleviating economic competition and providing for common defense (Spielmann 1994:51–52).

Judith Habicht-Mauche (1993, 1995) agreed with Spielmann's conclusions about the absence of elites in the northern Rio Grande, but for different reasons. In Habicht-Mauche's view, a combination of increased population density and the intensification of economic competition led to a system of alliances among entities she called "complex tribes." She based her study on an analysis of ceramics recovered from Arroyo Hondo Pueblo, in which she correlated stylistic diversity with structural changes in cultural diversity among fourteenth-century groups living in the northern Rio Grande region. These structural changes might have reflected emergent ethnic differentiation and more aggressive territorial maintenance that became manifested in regional exchange networks mediated by tribal institutions (Habicht-Mauche 1993:96). According to Habicht-Mauche, there were no elites, because none was needed to maintain what was, at least for a time, a relatively stable system.

Although the views of these scholars appear somewhat at odds, they have at least two things in common: a recognition that an evolutionary process resulted in the development of new organizational forms and a failure to specify the precise nature of the process that might have accounted for the complex patterns they describe. I hope to show how the application of architectural theory can enable researchers to reach beyond descriptions of social and architectural changes and explain what the changes mean or why they occurred.

Exploring the relationship between social and spatial organization is one way to approach cultural change. "Since architecture is sensitive to changes in spatial cognition, changes in architecture form are an expression of social and cultural change in terms of both symbolic and pragmatic use of space" (Plimpton and Hassan 1987:449). The implications for the northern Rio Grande are that the emergence of large, plaza-oriented pueblos reveals fundamental changes in attitudes, perceptions, and the use of space and that these behavioral changes are discoverable through an analysis of ancestral Pueblo architecture. Operating under the assumption that the settlement arrangements created by Pueblo societies were not random but embodied the social systems of those societies, I want to delve into and try to understand some fundamental principles underlying Pueblo spatial arrangements.

14

The application of spatial analysis techniques to architecture is not new (Brown 1990a:94), but such techniques have not been used intensively by archaeologists to test theories of organizational complexity. This is not to say that Southwestern archaeologists have ignored prehistoric architecture. On the contrary, commentators have written extensively about it for more than a hundred years. Lewis Henry Morgan (1881), Victor Mindeleff (1891), and T. Mitchell Prudden (1903) were early proponents of the need to investigate the relationship between architectural features and social organization. Others have discussed methodologies for relating the existence of discrete social groupings to specific architectural elements within Pueblo systems (Jackson 1954; Reed 1956; Rohn 1965; Wilcox 1975; Reynolds 1981; Dohm 1990; Lowell 1996). As one recent example, Julia Lowell (1996) relied on historically derived architectural correlates of moiety systems to identify a prehistoric moiety system at Turkey Creek Pueblo in Arizona. The architectural evidence for such descent groups was then used to create a model for social organization that was consistent with Gregory Johnson's (1983, 1989) concept of nested hierarchies (Lowell 1996:85–86). Irrespective of such efforts, even the best-documented and most extensive studies are often descriptive of the architecture itself (Creamer 1993; Morgan 1994) or of the nature of the relationship between cognizable social groups and definable architectural units (Wilcox 1975). Additional investigators have considered more ideational and symbolic explanations for spatial forms (Lekson 1981; Swentzell 1988, 1992; Saile 1990; Lipton 1992). Per Hage and Frank Harary (1983) even produced a detailed and much overlooked treatment of the potential uses of graph theory in the field of anthropology. Only recently has space syntax analysis been selected as a tool for mining more detailed organizational information from the vast and well-preserved record of prehistoric architecture (Bradley 1993; Clark 1995; Cooper 1995; Bustard 1996, 2003; Ferguson 1996; Shapiro 1997, 1999; Fangmeier 1998).

Although in this book I examine the physical structure of Arroyo Hondo Pueblo as a manifestation of its social structure, the ultimate significance of the research concerns the varying nature of human architectural responses to changing conditions throughout the Southwest. The ways in which Pueblo groups organized themselves and the manner in which these adjustments complemented changes in settlement patterns in risky and unpredictable environments have implications for a wide variety of times, places, and societies. The techniques of space syntax analysis can make a positive contribution to general anthropological theories regarding cultural development and change.

WHY PICK ON ARROYO HONDO PUEBLO?

One survey identified 124 ancestral Pueblo sites in the northern Rio Grande Valley that were occupied between 1325 and 1700 C.E. and had at least 50 rooms (Orcutt, Powers, and Van Zandt 1994). That figure constitutes the universe from which I chose a sample pueblo to test the efficacy of space syntax analysis. I selected Arroyo Hondo Pueblo because it has a well-documented record of excavation and was occupied during two separate and successive components during the Coalition and Classic periods.

The Arroyo Hondo project, a large, detailed, and relatively recent excavation, generated the kinds of data that permit the successful application of space syntax analysis. Recorded evidence of walls, doorways, and plazas at the site, where multiple roomblocks were occupied contemporaneously, enables one to discern patterns of access among the village's architectural units. Excavation revealed that people lived at Arroyo Hondo during two distinct components (figs. 2.2, 2.3) separated by approximately 25 to 30 years. The two occupations (1300–1345 and 1370–1425) straddle the interface between the Rio Grande Coalition (1200–1325) and Classic (1325–1600) periods. Because major changes in ancestral Pueblo demographics, social organization, and architecture took place during those periods, Arroyo Hondo seemed an excellent choice for testing a methodology that relates observable architectural forms to unobservable forms of social organization.

Unlike other settlements in what is now New Mexico, such as the pueblos of Pecos (Kidder 1958), Taos (Reynolds 1981), and San Marcos (Lycett 1994), which have long and sometimes complicated histories of successive construction and occupation, Arroyo Hondo's occupations are relatively well defined and dated through tree-ring and archaeomagnetic techniques (Creamer 1993:139–140, 156–164). Its built spaces (rooms and plazas) are well recorded, but even more important for space syntax purposes is the information the site yielded concerning room openings such as doorways, windows, and vents. Moreover, virtually all of the excavated rooms were categorized functionally, and

16

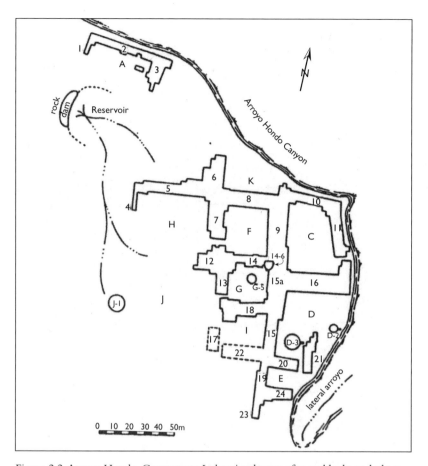

Figure 2.2. Arroyo Hondo, Component I, showing layout of roomblocks and plazas.

scores of tree-ring dates permitted the development of a settlement chronology (Creamer 1993:113–116). To the extent that its architectural variables can be controlled in order to investigate processes of cultural change in particular times and places, the Arroyo Hondo site may be unique in the Southwest.

No preexisting data set is perfect, however, and I consider several problems attendant upon the application of space syntax analysis to archaeological sites generally and ancestral Pueblo sites particularly. One problem, for example, involves the ability to separate discrete construction events from accretional growth. By way of illustration, when analyzing multicomponent sites, a potential for error exists when one

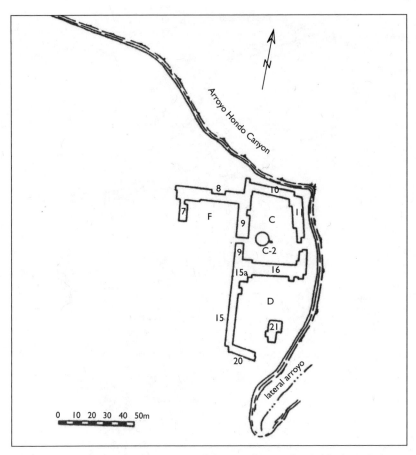

Figure 2.3. Arroyo Hondo, Component II, showing layout of roomblocks and plazas.

combines (for analytic purposes) a series of structures that were not occupied contemporaneously. Some building traditions are extremely persistent and produce enduring forms that are used for sequential occupations. Other architectural traditions develop over time, so that an examination at any particular point represents a snapshot that may not fully convey the historical contingencies that led to the ultimately observable built forms. Basically, the more precision one can apply to occupation chronologies, archaeological signatures, and structural abandonments, the more precise are the results obtained through space syntax analysis.

18

These issues ultimately touch on broader themes concerning the nature of the archaeological record and what is realistically recoverable. For example, in the absence of observable physical changes it is difficult to determine whether built space has been reconfigured according to social or ideological needs. Space syntax analysis cannot operate in a cultural vacuum, and the strength of its conclusions is always somewhat contingent upon what other sources of information can be brought to bear. I am unaware of any archaeological database that has been developed initially from the standpoint of space syntax analysis, and those who wield this tool are constrained by the availability of data that "fit" with the analytical methods. Fortunately, Arroyo Hondo Pueblo is a reasonably good fit.

Material culture is more than a simple text to be read, and the richness of the social fabric of life at Arroyo Hondo Pueblo cannot be gleaned entirely from walls, doorways, and plazas. Nonetheless, a quantifiable, syntactic approach can illuminate some ideas about life at the pueblo that are inaccessible through either traditional archaeological or cognitive approaches and yet may work in concert with both. I hope to illuminate both the static material elements that constitute the built environment and the dynamic properties of the spaces through which people moved and interacted. Space syntax analysis may not be the answer to every question, but it can provide some answers. To paraphrase a comment made by Jerry Moore in his book *Architecture and Power in the Ancient Andes* (1996), in the absence of informants to tell us the meaning of prehistoric architecture, we can still examine how buildings can create meaning, even if we do not know their precise meanings.

3

Arroyo Hondo Pueblo in the Context of Cultural Change

Space is filled with dramatic happenings.
—Rudolf Arnheim, "A Study in Spatial Counterpoint"

The following synthesis of events in the northern Rio Grande Valley, including a short history of Arroyo Hondo Pueblo, is intended not to be exhaustive but to provide the necessary context into which the insights provided by space syntax analysis can be placed. I summarize the changes in demographics, architecture, and organizational behavior that took place in the northern Rio Grande after 1300 C.E. and the ways in which those changes were reflected in the growth, development, and physical structure of Arroyo Hondo Pueblo.

DEMOGRAPHIC CHANGES

Archaeological evidence indicates that around 600 C.E., ancestral Pueblo groups began a shift toward sedentary agriculture, but no substantial population growth took place in the northern Rio Grande until sometime after 900 C.E. (Cordell 1984, 1989b:7–8). Between 900 and 1100, during the middle phase of the Rio Grande Developmental period, population increased and settlement expanded into areas that were more marginal for agriculture. As a result, by the late Developmental period, population had increased fourfold over earlier periods (Dickson 1979:71–72). The enduring question has been, Where did all those people come from? Ecological arguments in favor of local, indigenous population growth have been based on the tendency of organisms to fill up newly available niches as conditions become more agreeable. Favorable environmental changes, coupled with the exploitation of more drought-resistant and productive strains of maize that arrived in the northern Rio Grande sometime after 700 C.E. (Dickson 1975:72, 169), might have contributed to caloric stability and localized population increases, but the majority view attributes the population growth to post-Chacoan migration from the Mesa Verde or the Gallina area (Cameron 1995; Lekson and Cameron 1995; Crown, Orcutt, and Kohler 1996).

In trying to reconcile these views, archaeologists who have expressed support for a migration model, as well as those who rely on an indigenous development model, are faced with some problematic material facts. For example, to migration theorists, the presence of Mesa Verde–style ceramics in the northern Rio Grande region suggests that these items or the knowledge associated with their manufacture accompanied migrants as "cultural baggage." Indigenous growth theorists question the purported Mesa Verde connection or explain intrusive ceramics as being linked to imported water-control technologies or an associated form of ideological transfer (Dickson 1979:75). Furthermore, the indigenous expansion theorists point out that no site has been discovered in which a complete assemblage of material remains has revealed the presence of a wholly immigrant community (Habicht-Mauche 1993:86, quoting Cordell 1979:144, 1984:333). On the other hand, migrant groups generally do not bring their entire assemblages with them but attempt to blend in with their new host communities, and so perhaps it is unsurprising not to see unmistakable evidence of foreign site intrusion into the northern Rio Grande. Ultimately, the inferred population growth had a source, and if, in fact, a tenfold increase occurred between 1150 and 1250 C.E. (Cordell 1995:207), then it is instructive to note that there has never been a reported or observed case in which natural, in-place increases have accounted for such numbers (Crown, Orcutt, and Kohler 1996:193).

Tree-ring evidence reveals that during the thirteenth century—following the period of rapid population growth—the northern Rio Grande suffered from serious drought, which would have limited agricultural production and at least temporarily reduced the human carrying capacity. Some areas were abandoned, and people aggregated in areas where risk was minimized. Stated in a slightly different way, the drought caused an overall decline in productivity, but because it had the greatest effect on marginal regions, people relocated to the most predictable and, generally, well-watered areas. These ecological changes constitute one of several potential explanations for the dramatic population aggregation that became markedly evident late in the thirteenth century (Dickson 1975:169; Cordell, ed., 1980:9).

In 1995, the *Journal of Anthropological Archaeology* (vol. 14, no. 2) devoted an entire issue to migration throughout the Southwest. One is hard-pressed to find a consensus among the contributing scholars, except for the recognition that cultural factors such as warfare, factionalism, and the lure of larger settlements might have been as important as environmental factors in generating these movements. My goal is not to resolve the basic disputes among migration theorists; I merely take the position that, assuming the existence of substantial population movements, it is not unreasonable to infer the existence of some associated behavioral effects. Put simply, large-scale migrations affect social relations. "As a result of this external demographic pressure, new social and ethnic alliances would have been forged as these immigrants merged with the indigenous inhabitants of the northern Rio Grande to form large, aggregated settlements" (Habicht-Mauche 1993:6).

Psychologists who have studied migration have concluded that the process can cause physiological and psychological stress in both the migrating groups and the indigenous groups who absorb the newcomers. The former suffer the effects of social dislocation, and the latter feel crowded because of a real or perceived loss of control over their resources and immediate environment (Stokols 1976). One question is whether these behavioral stresses correlate with coping mechanisms such as architectural innovations, changes in the mechanisms for intergroup interaction, and an increased focus on territoriality as means of physically separating groups in order to diffuse tensions and reestablish a level of control (Bell, Fisher, and Loomia 1978). Aggregation was not a new phenomenon in the Southwest; for hundreds of years, many areas had experienced alternating periods of population aggregation

23

and dispersal (Cordell, Doyel, and Kintigh 1994). Nevertheless, the particular aggregations that began in the thirteenth century in the northern Rio Grande contributed to new kinds of architectural developments that are observable in sites such as Arroyo Hondo Pueblo.

By the beginning of the fifteenth century, population increase began to reverse as periods of intense drought contributed to the abandonment of all but the most productive and well-watered areas. The remaining pueblos, although fewer in number, continued as large, aggregated population centers. In other words, the population growth that began in the thirteenth century did not continue unabated but reversed gradually until the Spanish entrada, at which point the widely described effects of introduced diseases and social dislocation exacerbated the preexisting population decline (Dickson 1979; Ramenofsky 1987, 1990).

ARCHITECTURAL CHANGES

Assuming for the sake of argument that the weight of the evidence favors substantial population relocations from the Colorado Plateau and its environs to the Rio Grande Valley (Ahlstrom, Van West, and Dean 1995; Cameron 1995; Lipe 1995), the question to be considered is the relationship between demographic changes and architectural changes. During the thirteenth and fourteenth centuries, ancestral Pueblo settlement plans underwent one of the most radical changes since the pithouse-to-pueblo transition. By the thirteenth century, the ancestral Puebloans had ceased building Chaco-style great houses and had begun to construct pueblos consisting of hundreds or even thousands of rooms arranged in orthogonal roomblocks around multiple plazas. These large "plaza-roomblock" pueblos probably appeared first among the Western Pueblo groups (Adams 1991) but soon became predominant throughout the northern Southwest, persisting through the Classic period until contact with Spaniards resulted in additional architectural changes. A number of commentators have grappled with this shift in architectural style, as in these two examples:

> Then, for some reason, an urban urge resulted in the building of the great terraced communal structures covering many acres. It was these large villages that the Spanish explorers in 1540 first saw and called by the Spanish name pueblo, or village, in contrast to the temporary settlements of nomadic Indians. (Stubbs 1950:9–10)

24

Interpretation of the changes during the last few centuries in the Upper Rio Grande, from the front-directed Anasazi plan to the hollow-square layout (ubiquitous apparently during Pueblo IV), to predominance of parallel alignment, except among the Tewa, is beyond me. (Reed 1956:15–16)

Not all large settlements that developed during the Classic period had identical configurations. Some lacked central plazas, and others were composed of linear series of unconnected roomblocks separated by plaza-like spaces (see, generally, Morgan 1994). Nevertheless, the essential elements of this new kind of settlement pattern became adopted throughout the northern Southwest. The basic elements included multiple roomblocks, often multistoried and arranged orthogonally around one or more open plazas, each roomblock containing from a few dozen to more than 100 rooms. The authors of one review concluded that by around 1300 virtually all the inhabitants of the northern Rio Grande region were living in large, aggregated settlements (Crown, Orcutt, and Kohler 1996:201). Both Eastern and Western Pueblos built such plaza-centered villages, but after Spanish contact the plan was retained only by the Tewas; the pueblos of Nambe, Tesuque, and San Ildefonso represent the best surviving examples (Reed 1956:15; Swentzell 1988). Arroyo Hondo was one of the earliest pueblos to be constructed in this new style, though with approximately 1,000 rooms, it was far from the largest.[1]

On the basis of his studies of western pueblos, Charles Adams (1989, 1991, 1996) argued that the structural change to rectangular plazas enclosing kivas was preceded by social and organizational changes that enabled newly aggregated but diverse groups to live together peacefully. Adams offered the developing katsina cult as the operative mechanism but never conclusively resolved the "chicken-and-egg" question of whether the katsina cult or the large, plaza-centered pueblos came first. Inasmuch as social and organizational behaviors are more easily changed than the physical structures that contain them, one might intuitively favor the former. On the other hand, people have used structures in ways the original architects and builders never conceived of, so it might not be possible or even necessary to resolve this particular conundrum.

In a similar vein, Patricia Crown and Timothy Kohler (1990) considered correspondences between changes in population and the physical structuring of settlements. Using data from Pot Creek, a large, thirteenth- to fourteenth-century pueblo near Taos, New Mexico, they concluded that some structural changes actually began to appear prior to the largest population increases. These changes reinforced behavioral trends including increased use of plazas, greater differentiation of activity areas within plazas, single-episode roomblock construction, increased control of community and ritual areas, construction of more integrative facilities such as kivas, and changes in the sizes of residence units and rooms. According to Crown and Kohler, enclosing plazas would have served not only to restrict access and define group boundaries but also to strengthen the internal ties of the group or groups having access to particular plazas. They believed that plazas and kivas associated with particular roomblocks were related to the localized needs of households, whereas the main plaza was the site for activities of concern to the entire pueblo. The large kiva at Pot Creek was associated with even larger concerns, including the need to accommodate visitors from several outlying settlements.

Defensibility has been offered as a motivator for architectural change, and there is persuasive evidence for the existence of warfare throughout the northern Southwest before European contact (LeBlanc 1999). In addition to defensive architecture, the discovery of warrior-style symbolism in petroglyphs and kiva murals (Adams 1991), burned sites, and skeletal trauma all indicate increased conflict during the thirteenth and fourteenth centuries (Haas 1990; Wilcox and Haas 1994; Haas and Creamer 1996). Given this evidence, it is not surprising that a number of investigators have stressed the defensive nature of the large nucleated pueblos (e.g., Habicht-Mauche 1993).

If defensibility was so important, however, then one would expect to find these settlements in more defensible locations, which is not always the case. Nor do such settlements always incorporate the kinds of internal defensive arrangements, such as gates and parapets, that one might expect from an anxious or a threatened community. Nevertheless, by conjoining rooms into single, unitary structures, large pueblos were able to present the appearance of formidable and uniform walls.

ORGANIZATIONAL CHANGES

It should come as no great surprise that organizational changes took place in concert with demographic and architectural changes in

26

the northern Southwest. Probably the most notable development was the emergence and spread of the katsina cult. As described by Charles Adams (1991) and by Polly Schaafsma and Curtis Schaafsma (1974), this belief system operated as a device for social integration and conflict avoidance and was intimately associated with a variety of architectural innovations (Adams 1991).

How architecture was tied into the mechanisms that encouraged the growth of large, socially diverse settlements and how these communities might have melded into larger alliances (Habicht-Mauche 1993), such as that encompassing the users of the large kiva at Pot Creek Pueblo, are questions that have never been deeply investigated or resolved. If we assume, however, that the advent of large, multistoried, plaza-oriented pueblos was the architectural response to new demographic and economic stresses, then that development is consistent with Judith Habicht-Mauche's reading of patterns of ceramic diversity in the northern Rio Grande region at the time. She sees such patterns as markers of a tribal alliance system that served as a social coping mechanism in the face of new environmental and social stresses (Habicht-Mauche 1993:84–84, 87, 98, 1995:191–192).

A BRIEF HISTORY OF ARROYO HONDO PUEBLO

How does Arroyo Hondo Pueblo fit into the framework just outlined? The site lies approximately six miles south of Santa Fe, New Mexico, at an altitude of just over 7,000 feet in an area of piñon-juniper woodland (Kelley 1980; Rose, Dean, and Robinson 1981:xii, fig. 1). It covers an area of approximately 6.2 acres (Morgan 1994:219). The earliest part of the pueblo consisted of a roomblock oriented north-south along the western edge of a deep gorge branching off from the main arroyo, at the base of which was a permanent spring. Unlike the majority of the pueblo, which was built of adobe, the initial roomblock was constructed of masonry that probably was quarried from the western edge of the arroyo, several hundred yards from the pueblo site (Creamer 1993:14). Overall, the presence of dependable water and arable land probably contributed to the selection of the site for habitation. In addition to agricultural pursuits, the local residents participated in a variety of trading networks, both directly with local groups and indirectly with people as far away as the Pacific Coast for shells and northern Mexico for macaws (Habicht-Mauche 1993:xiii–xiv).

27

Figure 3.1. View of Arroyo Hondo site looking west from the shrine hill (neg. no. 128865, photograph by N. C. Nelson, courtesy Department of Library Services, American Museum of Natural History).

Following initial construction in the early 1300s, the pueblo underwent rapid expansion. By the mid-1330s, Arroyo Hondo Pueblo encompassed 24 roomblocks consisting of approximately 1,000 one- and two-story units clustered around ten plazas (Schwartz and Lang 1973: fig. 3.1). This occupation has been identified as Component I and was contemporaneous with occupations at other pueblos in the northern Rio Grande region, such as Tijeras, Puyé, and Paa-ko, all of which exhibited variations of orthogonal-roomblock, enclosed-plaza plans. The left side of figure 3.2 shows the final configuration of Component I as it appeared in the 1330s.

Soon after 1335 there is evidence for a decrease in precipitation (Rose, Dean, and Robinson 1981:100–104), which appears to have been coupled with a rapid decline in population at Arroyo Hondo. The latter development is suggested by an increase in the number of abandoned and trash-filled rooms, skeletal evidence of malnutrition and increased infant mortality, and a cessation of new construction (Palkovich 1980:29, 46–47). Wilma Wetterstrom, in a study of the plant remains from Arroyo Hondo, concluded that the drought was long and

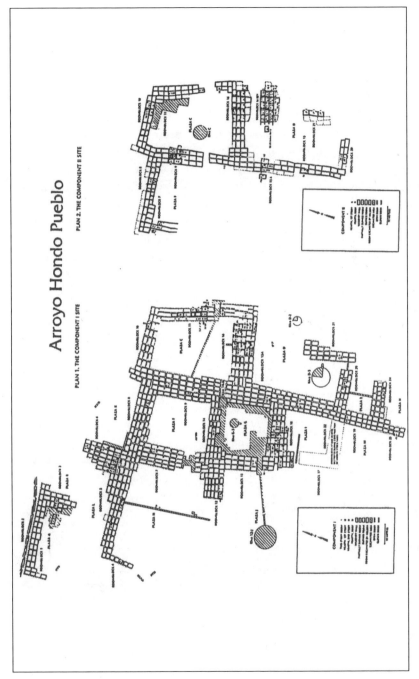

Figure 3.2. Detailed plans of Arroyo Hondo Pueblo, Components I and II.

severe enough to have substantially increased death rates, particularly among young children (Wetterstrom 1986:154–160).

Wetterstrom also inferred that drought conditions so reduced the age cohort born between 1335 and 1345 that organizational changes involving social and political rules might have been modified to accommodate the demographic realities of an altered social environment. In any event, it appears that the pueblo was virtually abandoned by around 1345. Portions may still have been occupied, possibly seasonally, by a small remnant population composed mainly of relatively old people (Wetterstrom 1986:143–146). A combination of tree-ring and skeletal studies suggested that declining precipitation and subsequent food shortages likely contributed to the exodus (Palkovich 1980), but it is not entirely clear why this abandonment took place. The single factor of reduced precipitation should not have completely precluded a continuation of agriculture. Other explanations such as deforestation, overhunting, and social stresses are potential candidates. But irrespective of the underlying reasons, this abandonment is considered to be the end of the Component I occupation of the site.

Arroyo Hondo remained essentially unoccupied for at least two decades. During the 1370s a period of new construction began that is correlated with a climatic regime of slightly above-average rainfall (Rose, Dean, and Robinson 1981:100–104). This second phase, identified as Component II (fig. 3.2), was built on top of the ruins of the original pueblo but was much less extensive, being composed of only about 200 single-story rooms in nine roomblocks arranged around three plazas (Creamer 1993:4). Compared with late-fourteenth-century communities in other parts of the northern Rio Grande Valley, this second-phase settlement was a relatively small village. For example, the pueblos of Kuaua (with more than 1,200 rooms), Poshuouinge (with more than 2,000 rooms), and Sapawe (with more than 4,400 rooms) were all occupied during Arroyo Hondo's Component II (Morgan 1994:205, 213, 215). This is not to imply that these other pueblos were fully constructed or occupied during the 1370s but only that the Component II reoccupation at Arroyo Hondo took place at a time when some truly enormous pueblos were being built. The point is that Component II constituted a comparatively small part of a social landscape increasingly dominated by much larger towns (Habicht-Mauche 1993:7).

Archaeological evidence, primarily in the form of ceramics,

revealed contacts between Arroyo Hondo and a number of other settlements during this phase and supported theories of interaction based on long-distance trade and craft specialization. Habicht-Mauche (1993:85–95) viewed evidence of increased ceramic specialization and standardization, together with evidence of widespread trade, as an indicator of changes in social organization that developed between the Coalition and Classic periods. She described these changes in terms of an evolution of complex tribes, but there is no indication that the process was controlled or driven by the existence of any elite elements in the society (Habicht-Mauche 1993:94, 1995:192). That substantial portions of both the everyday culinary ware and the decorated ware collected at Arroyo Hondo have been found to have originated at other pueblos strengthens the argument in favor of intraregional trading networks, but how such trade was directed is still unclear.

The cycle of drought that may have contributed to the first abandonment returned to the northern Rio Grande in the late 1300s and early 1400s, peaking at around 1420 (Rose, Dean, and Robinson 1981: 100, 104). Archaeological evidence suggests that sometime between 1415 and 1420, a large fire that might have been the result of raiding or warfare destroyed a substantial portion of Arroyo Hondo Pueblo (LeBlanc 1999:234). These double disasters undoubtedly contributed to the final abandonment of the village, which took place sometime before 1425. This abandonment coincided with a general population decline in the northern Rio Grande at a time when climatic factors were contributing to decreases in agricultural productivity and groups were aggregating in more productive areas. Following this second abandonment, the Arroyo Hondo site was never reoccupied.

AN OVERVIEW OF ARROYO HONDO'S ARCHITECTURE

The architecture of Arroyo Hondo Pueblo has been comprehensively described (Beal 1971, 1972; Creamer 1993), but an overview is appropriate to link what is already understood about the architecture with the new information provided by space syntax analysis.

Arroyo Hondo was built as a "puddled adobe" pueblo.[2] Its enclosed-plaza layout looks very much like a preconceived architectural plan. Roomblocks were built at right angles to one another in ways that created important, nonarchitectural plaza spaces. The suggestion of community-level organization gains support from sources as diverse as

Figure 3.3. Men at work on Building II, Arroyo Hondo Pueblo (neg. no. 128868, photograph by N. C. Nelson, courtesy Department of Library Services, American Museum of Natural History).

tree-ring cutting dates and the nature of wall abutments that illustrate when and how certain portions of the pueblo were built (Creamer 1993:12). The evidence shows that a number of roomblocks in both components began with the construction of two long, parallel walls that were subdivided into small rooms by shorter cross walls (fig. 3.3). Buildings constructed in this style have been called "ladder structures" (Roney 1996:150) and "spine buildings" (Dean 1996:38). The style is not unique to Arroyo Hondo but is associated with a number of large, contemporaneous settlements (Cordell 1996:234–235).

The ability to discern community-based conceptual planning at Arroyo Hondo is important for space syntax analysis. It implies that the structure of space at this and other, similarly situated pueblos can be analyzed as a unit because it represents a shared, preconceived view of the built environment rather than individual, situational decision making by the inhabitants.

The hollow-square, plaza-and-roomblock pueblos exemplified by Arroyo Hondo appeared in the northern Rio Grande by the late 1200s or possibly earlier (Reed 1956:14). Although the concept of plaza-

Figure 3.4. Aerial view of Arroyo Hondo Pueblo, ca. 1970s (photograph by David Grant Noble, School of American Research Arroyo Hondo Collections).

oriented construction was neither new nor uniquely associated with the northern Southwest (Jackson 1954; Reed 1956; Low 1995), the rapidity with which this style was adopted has made it the subject of numerous inquiries. Some archaeologists have attempted to relate the nature of plaza-oriented settlements to a group's ability to respond to social or demographic changes. For example, Victor Mindeleff saw the pueblos as reflective of the overall Hopi system:

> The constant movement of the tribe, due to the use of outlying farming settlements...has its analog within each village, where there is an equally constant movement from house to house and from row to row. The clans which inhabit a village are combined into larger units or groups known as phratries; locally such clans are said to "belong together." In the olden days each phratry occupied its own quarters in the village, its own cluster or row, as the case might be, and while the custom is now much broken down, just how far it ceased to exercise its influence is yet to be determined. (Mindeleff 1891:646–647)

33

Charles Adams has tied the idea of an enclosed plaza to the spread of the katsina cult through the Southwest (Adams 1989, 1991), although this may be a case in which the adoption of architectural design changes preceded the organizational and ritual changes associated with the katsina cult and preadapted the pueblos to incorporate it. Alternatively, such architectural innovation might merely have followed the social and religious developments associated with the cult itself and been more related to the large population increases that characterized the region (Habicht-Mauche 1993:5–6).

With reference to Arroyo Hondo's interior design, excavations in the 1970s revealed that plazas were the settings for a wide variety of domestic and religious activities. The presence of both large and small kivas in the plazas indicates the importance of these areas for the inhabitants. Indeed, the plazas probably served the same functions for the populace that Bill Hillier and Julienne Hanson attribute to streets and thoroughfares in modern cities, namely, that of providing opportunities for social interactions (Hillier, Penn, et al. 1993). Winifred Creamer (1993:110) classified rooms at Arroyo Hondo according to their functions, recognizing, among a total of eight broad categories, habitation rooms, storage rooms, ceremonial rooms, and ceremonial-storage rooms. Unlike the case for the ethnographically derived Hopi model, in which rooms may be distinguished in part by their size, the relatively uniform sizes of rooms at Arroyo Hondo (6–8 square meters each) suggest that there was little or no correlation between size and function.

Creamer (1993) recognized three residence patterns in the Component I architecture. First and predominant were two-room, single-story residence units. Second and also appearing in significant numbers were two-story units of two to five rooms each; these included examples in which new rooms were built onto existing structures. Third, some two-story, three-room spaces were planned and built as single structures (Beal 1972; Creamer 1993:122–123).

Component II was composed entirely of single-story roomblocks with rooms slightly smaller than those of Component I. Whether these differences resulted from shortages of raw materials or from other cultural choices is not entirely clear (Creamer 1993:41–42). There is a consistency in that the majority of residence units in both phases were made up of one or two rooms, but Component I exhibits a higher percentage of multiroom units than Component II (Creamer 1993:130–131). Despite some minor distinctions, Creamer's comments are

34

generally consistent with earlier reports by John D. Beal, who found that whereas Classic-period rooms were typically composed of two rooms, the earlier Coalition-period residential units were often composed of three or more rooms (Beal 1971:67, 69, 1972:92). These differences might signal a shift of household residence from extended family units to nuclear family units. If this type of change can be demonstrated, it could imply a greater focus on smaller family units and greater reliance on non-kinship-based forms of social integration. As I describe in chapter 5, the application of space syntax analysis to Components I and II supports such a hypothesis.

Doorways are important architectural features that are critical for space syntax analysis because they help to delineate access patterns. Approximately 85 doorways or their remains were identified among the 150 excavated rooms at Arroyo Hondo Pueblo (Beal 1972; Creamer 1993:113–116; fig. 3.5).[3] As shown in table 3.1, there are differences in the numbers and conditions of doorways constructed during the two occupations.

Although many of the excavated rooms had no doorways and presumably were accessed via ceiling entries, a number of Component I rooms had two or even three doorways. The majority of these doorways were found sealed, although whether the sealing occurred at the time of abandonment or at some earlier time is difficult to determine. Beal suggested that the sealing of doorways was sometimes related to construction practices. He noted that sealing "reflects a change from horizontal to vertical residence units, at least in relation to ground-story rooms" (Beal 1972:90). To the extent that the sealing treatment appears to match the method of wall construction (e.g., Creamer 1993:27, fig. 2.10), one could conclude that sealing took place at the completion of the construction episode, but such information is not readily available (Cooper 1995:162). The relationship of open and sealed doorways to ancestral Pueblo building practices might relate to population increases that necessitated the construction of second-story residence units, with the result that lower-story rooms were converted to storage or other alternative functions (Cooper 1995:162).

Creamer (1993:122) discussed several potential reasons for sealing doorways, including changes in the size of residence groups, construction practices that required temporary entries, and a shift from nuclear to extended-family social organization. Creamer and Beal each recognized a physical component (the functional process of sealing) and a

35

Figure 3.5. Doorway in the southern wall of room 3, Building XX, looking south (neg. no. 2A23684, photograph by N. C. Nelson, Courtesy Department of Library Services, American Museum of Natural History).

social component (changes in social relationships that accompanied the sealing), but neither author expressly discussed the possibility of seasonal blocking (Cooper 1995:162). For example, Mindeleff (1891:183), in his comments on Zuni architecture, observed: "Doorways closed with masonry are seen in many ruins. Possibly these are an indication of the temporary absence of the owner, as in the harvest season, or at the time of destruction or abandonment of the village; but they may have been closed for the purpose of economizing warmth and fuel during the winter season."

It may be that the reasons for blocking individual doorways cannot be discerned, but the problem that doorways pose for space syntax

TABLE 3.1

Summary of Doorway Construction,
Arroyo Hondo Components I and II

Component	Excavated Rooms	Rooms with Single Door	Rooms with Multiple Doors	No. Sealed Doors
I	100	20	23	18
II	50	14	0	4

Source: Adapted from Creamer 1993:113–116, Appendix C.

analysis relates to the need to establish chronological control over access routes between spaces. Space syntax analysis posits that social relationships are embodied in architectural features, as in whether or not a doorway between two residence units is open, thus either permitting or prohibiting social interchange between the two spaces. The ability to infer such relationships depends on what is known about the status of the doorway at the time the spaces were occupied.

Judging from the available information, it appears that Component I residence units were generally more accessible from a variety of other units than were Component II units. More than 40 percent of the excavated Component I rooms had evidence of doorways, and more than half of these rooms had multiple doorways. Not only were there fewer doorways per unit during the Component II occupation, but none of the excavated rooms associated with this period revealed the existence of multiple doorways. Assuming that Creamer was correct about some doorways being added as needed only during periods of construction, we still have no explanation for the presence of multiple doorways during Component I.

Despite the apparent cultural continuity between the two occupations (Creamer 1993:56), some noticeable differences existed in their architectural arrangements. For example, besides the absence of rooms with multiple doorways, no ceremonial rooms were identified from the Component II excavations. Whether this absence of ceremonial spaces is an artifact of excavation is speculative, but inasmuch as almost 25 percent of the Component II rooms were excavated (and almost 50 percent of roomblock 16), the probability that all the ceremonial spaces were simply missed appears low. Descriptions of architectural features have traditionally served as a basis for comparing structures within sites, but that approach is limited by problems of subjectivity and consistency among different researchers. Space syntax analysis provides a different and more quantifiable way to understand the nature of these spatial contrasts.

CONCLUSION

The Coalition and Classic periods were times of variation and synthesis in the northern Rio Grande Valley. Irrespective of whether the growth of settlements is attributable to interregional or intraregional migration or to localized population increases, Arroyo Hondo is representative of the new kinds of communities that accommodated groups of people who had not previously lived together and that encouraged additional material and organizational changes. Among the unanswered questions is why these changes occurred, and one of the ways in which this question might be answered involves considering how space was organized in these settlements. The evidence suggests the existence of a common spatial syntax that underlies all late Pueblo settlement structure and design, although it might not have been expressed in precisely the same manner throughout the ancestral Pueblo world. Local cultural and environmental differences undoubtedly contributed to the variety of individual forms observed among late prehistoric and historic settlements (Morgan 1994), but until the underlying syntax is investigated, the issue remains moot. If social information resides in settlement design, then an analysis of representative sites such as Arroyo Hondo Pueblo may help to explain the relationship between the architectural record and the archaeological record.

4

A Primer on
Space Syntax Analysis

*The concept of space then, once defined by geometric principles through
various formations of points, straight lines, and planes,
now is replaced by a study of relations.*
—Rudolf Carnap, "Space"

In this chapter I offer an introduction to the theory, methods, and archaeological applicability of space syntax analysis. Although at first blush the techniques appear complicated, the process is relatively straightforward and has many potential archaeological applications (Foster 1989; Bonanno et al. 1990a; Brown 1990b; Fairclough 1992; Osman 1993; Banning 1996; Osman and Suliman 1996). Space syntax analysis connects built forms and social organization through the idea that societies arrange space in accordance with the same rules that govern their social arrangements, in what G. Ankerl (1981:43) calls a "spatial sociology."

One way in which societies communicate social information through spatial manipulation is by generating unwritten social rules that control the ways in which small architectural elements are joined together to form larger units, in much the way words are joined to express ideas in a conventional language. Just as all languages look and

39

sound different from one another but share the concept of a grammatical structure, so, too, does each culture create its unique architectural arrangements according to an underlying and unstated spatial grammar. Any observer can see the architecture, but the syntactic structure is hidden and not immediately apparent. Space syntax analysis allows one to decouple the most fundamental aspects of space usage from all the attendant cultural noise and reveal the underlying syntax that created the spatial connections that compose the built environment.

THEORETICAL FOUNDATIONS

People deploy themselves in and modify space in patterned ways, all of which have social meanings. As an example of how one might infer process from pattern, consider an army camp. An army may relocate from place to place, but its "fingerprint" is always produced by the placement of tents, mobile buildings, and facilities in a consistent format. The overall arrangement carries information that can reveal social structures and relationships, patterns of activity, and even ideology (Hillier and Hanson 1984:39). Space syntax analysis provides a tool with which to recognize and investigate those patterns.

The foundations of space syntax analysis are firmly anchored in the branch of mathematics known as graph theory. I offer the following descriptions in order to demystify some of the logic behind space syntax calculations and reveal the genesis of some of the jargon used by the theory's developers. In describing the spatial properties of networks composed of nodes and linkages, E. J. Taaffe and H. L. Gauthier (1973: 101) discussed two measures of the spatial properties of such networks: a connectivity measure, which describes the total, aggregate geometrical pattern of the entire network, and an accessibility measure, which describes the relationship of the individual elements to the entire network. Connectivity is a structural property of networks that reveals the degree of interconnection among their nodes. It can be applied synchronically, as between two different networks, or diachronically, as between different stages in a single network. Connectivity is not merely a descriptive term but one that can be presented graphically, as illustrated in figure 4.1, as well as mathematically.

Network A in figure 4.1 consists of six nodes connected by five linkages. Inasmuch as there is only one sequence of linkages between any two nodes, this network is minimally connected. Network B also

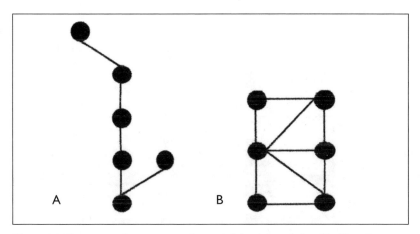

Figure 4.1. Two contrasting patterns of connectivity. Adapted from Taaffe and Gauthier 1973:102.

consists of six nodes, but each of them is linked to the others in more than one way, which results in a total of nine linkages. Clearly, network B is structurally more complex than network A, and there are formulas that can put numbers on these differences. One measure, the gamma index, is the ratio of the number of actual linkages in a network to the maximum possible number of linkages (Taaffe and Gauthier 1973:102). It is expressed by the formula

$$\text{gamma} = \frac{e}{3 \times (n - 2)}$$

where e is the actual number of linkages in a system, n is the number of nodes, and $3(n - 2)$ is the potential number of linkages if every node were connected to every other. Using this formula, network A in figure 4.1 has a value of approximately 0.42 (5/12), and network B has a value of 0.75 (9/12). In comparison with a situation in which every node is interconnected (12/12 = 1.00), network A is 42 percent connected and network B is 75 percent connected. In other words, the first network has a connectivity value that is only 55 percent of the value of the second network; it is slightly more than half as connected.

To illustrate these concepts in a real-world scenario, consider figure 4.2, which is a cross section of a three-story residential structure at Acoma Pueblo, based on drawings prepared by the Historic American Buildings Survey in 1934 (United States Department of the Interior 1934). Figure 4.3 shows a network consisting of 11 nodes (built spaces)

41

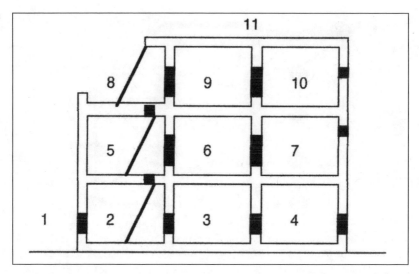

Figure 4.2. Longitudinal section of a three-story residential structure at Acoma Pueblo (Block 6, Unit 4). Adapted from United States Department of the Interior 1934, sheet 79.

and 11 linkages (doors, hatchways) that results from the transformation of figure 4.2 into a schematic form used in space syntax analysis. Each space is numbered in order to clarify its position within the network (space number 1 is the outdoors, from which one could enter both rooms 2 and 4). Application of the gamma index formula to this room-block reveals that there are 27 potential linkages (3[11–2] = 27), but only 11 actual linkages. Therefore, the degree of connectivity (the gamma index itself) is approximately 0.41 (11/27 = 0.4074), which indicates a relatively segregated network. In other words, access is controlled, and there are few, if any, alternative paths through the structure. Alone these figures provide little insight into the people responsible for the construction, but they do reveal how architectural spaces can be schematically transformed and quantified. The practical uses of such quantification will be seen in connection with the description of space syntax analysis.

Networks composed of nodes that are more than minimally linked typically include one or more alternative paths between nodes. These paths are called *circuits*, which are defined as finite, closed paths in which the initial node of the linkage sequence coincides with the ter-

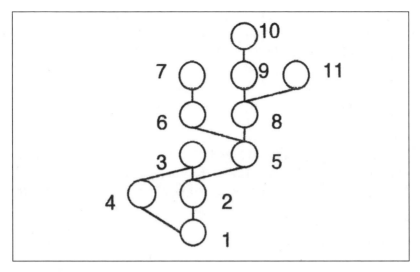

Figure 4.3. Network, or "justified access," graph for the Acoma Pueblo roomblock shown in figure 4.2.

minal node (Taaffe and Gauthier 1973:104). The number of alternative paths, or circuits, can be measured by calculating the number of linkages those paths add to a minimally connected network. This measure of circuitry, the alpha index, is the ratio of the number of actual circuits in a network to the maximum possible number (Taaffe and Gauthier 1973:104). The alpha index is expressed mathematically as

$$\text{alpha index} = \frac{e - (n + 1)}{2 \times n - 5}$$

where, again, e is the actual number of linkages and n is the number of nodes. Alpha index values range from zero for a minimally connected network to 1.00 for a maximally connected network. For the networks illustrated in figure 4.1, the alpha index for network A is 0 ([5 − 6 + 1]/[2(6) − 5] = 0/7), because there are no circuits, and for network B it is 0.57 ([9 − 6 + 1]/[2(6) − 5] = 4/7). Network B is clearly more connected than A, but it is not maximally connected, which would require 12 circuits. For the Acoma Pueblo roomblock shown in figures 4.2 and 4.3, the alpha index is approximately 0.06 ([11 − (11 − 1)]/[2(11) − 5] = 1/17), because it has only a single, shallow circuit.

There is a practical side to the foregoing discussion, because a number of archaeologists have utilized elements of graph theory in their research. For example, M. Hopkins (1987) used accessibility diagrams to analyze several compounds at the site of Teotihuacan in the Valley of Mexico. Hopkins found significant numerical differences in accessibility measurements that appeared to reflect functional differences. Thus, "palaces," or structures ostensibly associated with elite activities, had relatively restricted and controlled patterns of access in comparison with more public compounds, or those associated with non-elite activities, which had less restricted and more highly circuited patterns of access (Hopkins 1987:395-397). Although not employing as unified an approach as a formal application of space syntax analysis, Hopkins's research demonstrated how graph theory can help to unravel spatial patterns and reveal social patterns that might not otherwise be discernible.

Jerry Moore (1992, 1996) applied a variation of access analysis to a series of *ciudadelas* at the Chimu site of Chan Chan in Peru in order to test a functional explanation for a specific architectural element described as a "U-shaped room." Moore based his approach on elements from both graph theory and locational geography (Moore 1992:102), and although he did not explicitly employ space syntax analysis, his use of "line-of-site" graphs was an acknowledged modification of some space syntax concepts (Moore 1992:104). Despite some problems in controlling for occupational contemporaneity, including the assumption rather than the demonstration that sealed doorways were post-abandonment phenomena, Moore's use of access graphs revealed that the traditional view of U-shaped rooms—that they served an administrative function by controlling access to storerooms—was insupportable (Moore 1992:110). This inference was based on a series of quantitative measurements that appeared to contravene traditional archaeological explanations but that could not be made without some reference to a preexisting body of archaeological data. Even though neither Hopkins nor Moore relied specifically on space syntax analysis, both acknowledged its importance as a developing technique.

THE METHODOLOGY OF SPACE SYNTAX ANALYSIS

Space syntax analysis offers techniques for the "representation and quantification of spatial patterns" (Orhun, Hillier, and Hanson 1995). More specifically, it is concerned with topological relationships within buildings or settlements, rather than with attributes such as size, construction methods, and stylistic details.[1] According to space syntax theory, the structured topological elements mesh two types of social interactions: those among the inhabitants of a structure or settlement and those between inhabitants and visitors (Hillier, Hanson, and Peponis 1987:217).

The physical organization of built space is not random but embodies both the institutions and social structures of societies: "It is generally clear that human social behavior has evolved in parallel with the evolution of material culture in general, and of architectural culture in particular. It follows, therefore, that we should not expect to understand the forms of social behavior that relate to architecture without considering the possibility that they have been affected by the development of architecture itself" (Hillier and Hanson 1987:198).

Given that assumption, the first step in the process is to reduce built elements to four simplified forms: enclosed spaces, open spaces, boundaries, and openings. These elements are combined with four additional structural concepts—symmetry, asymmetry, distributedness, and nondistributedness—to produce the fundamental configurational relationships illustrated in figure 4.4.

In space syntax terms, *symmetry* refers to the accessibility relationship of two spaces. In situations in which the spatial relationship of A to B is the same as that of B to A, then those spaces are symmetrically related. As a general rule, symmetrical relationships tend to have higher degrees of accessibility than do asymmetrical relationships, which tend toward greater isolation.

The concept of *distributedness* refers to the potential for movement within a system, including whether one space controls access to another space. If such control is present, in the sense that one can enter space A only by going through space B, then the relationship is nondistributed. Alternatively, distributed spaces are found in networks in which there are multiple access routes, so no single space controls accessibility between spaces (Cooper 1995:70–71).

By treating all spaces as equally significant, space syntax analysis eliminates the cultural biases inherent in architectural descriptions that conflate function and value, such as "family room" and "guest room." Each defined space is analyzed in terms of its links to every other space in the network, including the outside surrounding space, which is referred to as the *carrier space* or *root*.[2] Using this approach, large plaza

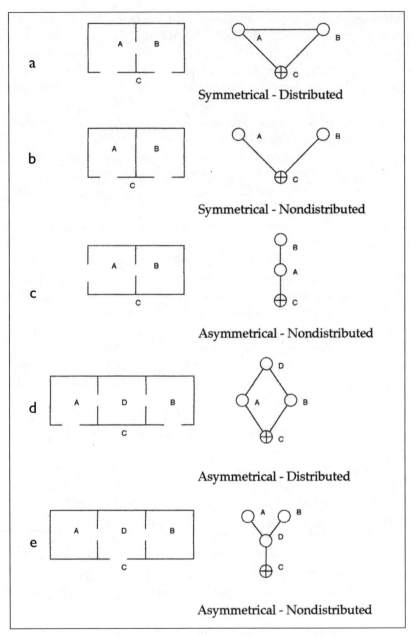

Figure 4.4. The fundamental configurational relationships of architectural units as conceptualized in space syntax analysis. Adapted from Hillier and Hanson 1984:148–149.

spaces are given the same value as small storage rooms, because the focus of space syntax is on the manner in which built space is structured, not on how it is used. In some respects, space syntax analysis is analogous to pure mathematical models, in that both provide unadorned views of fundamental, patterned relationships. It is assumed that social systems create spaces to either encourage or discourage contacts between inhabitants (persons inside the system who control access) and strangers (persons outside the system who may enter but whose access is otherwise controlled). The degree of spatial encouragement or discouragement conveys something about the "openness" of the system. Beneath the calculations, what is really being analyzed is a proxy measure of potential social interaction.

Perhaps the fundamental question concerning such interaction is, How difficult or easy is it for one to move through a system in order to interact with other people? Stated in space syntax terms the question is, How well integrated is the system? Any structure may be defined according to the number of interior spaces that must be crossed to reach the carrier, or surrounding external space. Systems in which many spaces must be traversed are considered "deep," and those with few spaces to be crossed are defined as "shallow." Depth is determined by the arrangement of spaces relative to the carrier. In figure 4.4, diagrams a and b both have depths of 1, whereas diagrams c, d, and e all have depths of 2. Depth becomes important in calculating a key variable, the "integration value."

Although Hillier, Hanson, and their colleagues have developed several measures with which to analyze spatial configurations, perhaps the most useful is the one called "real relative asymmetry," which not only measures the accessibility of a system but also takes into account variations in systems of different sizes. For ease in understanding the applicable concepts, and for consistency with some of the group's more recent writings (Orhun, Hillier, and Hanson 1995), I refer to this term as the *integration value*. It describes the relationship of each space to all others within the entire network. The integration value is calculated as $2(d-1)/k-2$, where d is the mean depth of all spaces from the carrier and k is the total number of spaces in a justified graph that describes the network.[3] Mean depth is calculated by assigning a depth value to each space based on the number of steps needed to reach it from the carrier, then summing these values and dividing the sum by the number of spaces in the system, less one (to account for the original space).

This portion of the analysis is called "deriving the grammar of a site."

Justified access graphs (fig. 4.5, see fig. 4.3) are graphic illustrations of the permeability of a spatial system (Orhun, Hillier, and Hanson 1995:470). Spaces are represented by circles, and paths are represented by lines that begin with the carrier space. Each space is aligned, or "justified," according to the number of intermediate spaces needed to reach the carrier. Spaces that are the same distance from the carrier—that is, at the same depth—are placed in the same horizontal row.

Calculating integration values provides a continuum of values in which smaller numbers—those less than 1.00 and approaching zero—indicate greater integration and larger numbers—those greater than 1.00—indicate greater segregation. The integration measure is considered the most important with which to gauge the spatial relations in a system (Chapman 1990:80; Hillier, Penn, et al. 1993), and it is the measure I use throughout the rest of this study. There is no theoretical maximum number. A single chain of 20 linked spaces has a mean integration value of 2.96, while the twentieth space has a value of 4.44. Increasing the depth of the chain to 50 linked spaces raises the mean integration value to 5.00, and the fiftieth space has a value of 7.50.

Empirical studies have revealed that contemporary European and North American settlements tend to have higher integration values than traditional non-Western settlements, but the values obtained through this formula are all relative. Thus, an integration value of 0.95, taken alone, does not necessarily imply the existence of a society that is more or less complex in any absolute sense. Instead, it suggests a society in which spatial activity is relatively integrated and in which social interaction is potentially very open. In contrast, a system of similar size with an integration value of 1.35 might be expected to exhibit many fewer manifestations of accessibility and greater internal differentiation and to be generally more highly controlled than the settlement with the lower value.

Integration values are quantitative expressions of justified access graphs (Orhun, Hillier, and Hanson 1995:476). Their significance is that different integration values imply differences in social relations in space. Deep spaces segregate, in the sense that they isolate themselves from the rest of the complex. Shallow spaces integrate, in the sense that they operate as unifying elements for the entire complex. Despite the existence of different, culturally distinct spatial arrangements, underlying principles reveal how functional patterns may appear in different cultural settings. For example, increasing the average depth from a particular space to all other spaces is one way to achieve greater segregation of selected categories of spaces for social purposes. This can be physically accomplished in a number of ways, including the placement of architectural barriers to restrict access and direct movement.

Consider figure 4.5, in which four buildings have identical arrangements of adjacent spaces but in which openings have been varied to facilitate or retard movement. The nature of the connections and potential movements is illustrated with justified access graphs that reveal d as the most segregated network and c as the most integrated network. Graphs a and b have the same moderately segregated value, despite their different access patterns. That a has a relatively shallow, tree-branching form, whereas b has a deeper, three-ring pattern, illustrates the potential problem of relying on a numerical value without considering the form of the network from which it was derived. In addition, although the average values are the same, the distribution of values is much different, with b having a greater range and variability.

Another important aspect of space syntax analysis is illustrated in table 4.1. Calculating the integration values for each space in a building produces a hierarchy of values for the entire network. Rather than merely noting that a space is either "open and accessible" or "restricted and segregated," one can determine just how accessible a space is relative to the rest of its network. In other words, space syntax analysis is much more sensitive to the kinds of subtle distinctions that are seldom discerned through empirical observations of ruins, maps, or site plans.

Examining table 4.1 in conjunction with figure 4.5, one can see how the rearrangement of openings may substantially change particular values, as in the case of room 5, or have no effect at all, as in the case of room 3. Further, in building d, room 3 has the lowest value of all the rooms, whereas in building c it has a higher position. It is this continuum of values, when combined with a functional analysis of the built spaces, that permits one to draw inferences about the relationships between the spatial and the social.

An actual example of the foregoing discussion is Laurel Cooper's study of Chacoan great houses (1995). Most archaeologists who have investigated Chacoan architecture have concentrated on masonry styles and architectural forms without considering the arrangement and permeability of spaces within contemporaneously occupied great houses. One aspect of Cooper's research was its demonstration that even

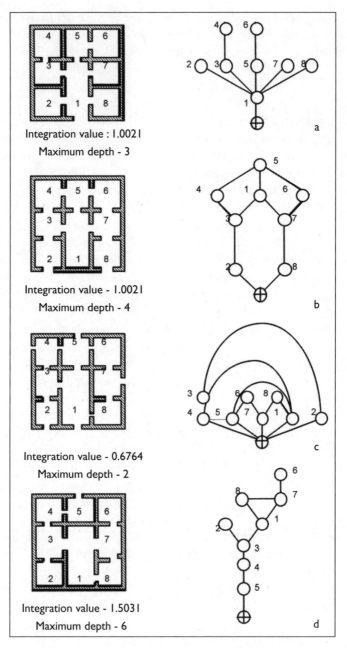

Figure 4.5. Examples of justified access graphs (right) for identical configurations of spaces with different patterns of openings.

TABLE **4.1**

Network Accessibility Values for the Justified Access Graphs
Shown in Figure 4.5

Space	Graph A	Graph B	Graph C	Graph D
Carrier	1.015	1.240	0.338	2.480
1	0.226	0.676	0.451	0.902
2	1.015	1.127	0.902	1.578
3	0.789	0.789	0.789	0.789
4	1.578	1.127	0.676	1.127
5	0.789	1.015	0.451	1.691
6	1.578	1.127	0.902	2.142
7	1.015	0.789	0.676	1.353
8	1.015	1.127	0.902	1.466

though the overall building styles of several great houses appeared similar, genuine internal differences existed between them that became apparent through space syntax analysis. For example, Pueblo del Arroyo revealed evidence of rebuilding and remodeling, with each of two sections exhibiting some "ringiness" and one having deeper and more segregated spaces. ("Rings" are circulation pathways involving more than two spaces, and ringiness is a measure of the number of rings in a system. A high ringiness value suggests that a sytem is well distributed [Hillier and Hanson 1984: 107].) Salmon Ruin, on the other hand, was built in a single, planned episode and exhibited a branching pattern with strong emphasis on front-to-back movement and deep, segregated spaces. A third example, Aztec Ruin, also appeared to emphasize depth and segregation. Obviously, Chacoan great houses were separated from Arroyo Hondo in both time and place, but the idea that ostensibly similar appearances can mask different patterns of internal access is fundamental to the kinds of arrangements discovered at Arroyo Hondo.

In addition to describing the relationships of individual spaces to the system as a whole, space syntax analysis quantifies the relationships between individual adjacent spaces (Hillier and Hanson 1984:108 −109). The attribute of *control* is a local measure that identifies spaces that are significant in directing the accessibility of neighboring spaces.

The control measure, E, is calculated by creating a justified access graph and counting the number of neighbors of each space—the spaces with which it has direct connections. Each space gives to its neighbors a value equal to $1/n$ of its "control." The control value of any space is determined by summing all the fractional values of the neighboring spaces (Hillier and Hanson 1984:109). For example, in figure 4.5a, space 1 is connected to five other spaces plus the carrier space. The control value for space 1 is 5.00 $(1 + 1 + 1 + 1 + 1)$. On the other hand, space 2, which is connected to only space 1, has a control value of 0.167; that is, it receives only 1/6 of space 1's connections. A visual observation of figure 4.5a easily identifies space 1 as a controlling space, but calculating control values permits analysis and comparison of larger structures with numerous spaces. Spaces with high control values—those in excess of 1.00—have direct connections to many neighboring spaces, as well as the potential to control accessibility. Spaces with control values of less than 1.00 are not well connected to their neighbors and have only weak control over adjacent spaces.

ISSUES ARISING FROM THE APPLICATION OF SPACE SYNTAX ANALYSIS

Despite a variety of critiques during the past three decades (Leach 1978; Brown 1990a; Osman and Suliman 1994, 1995), the essential efficacy of space syntax analysis remains solid. It is a tool that can be applied in certain situations and that, when used in concert with other tools, can tell us things about how people arrange their spaces and their societies.

Very early on, Edward Leach (1978) asserted that space syntax relied on an oversimplified and reductionist view of space that eliminated all descriptive characteristics. Leach was correct that spaces may have culturally defined meanings that space syntax cannot retrieve. That an ancestral Pueblo kiva was located in the middle of a plaza does not mean that it was equally accessible to all inhabitants of the surrounding roomblocks. Social restrictions may exist that are not manifested in physical remains. In one sense, by eliminating from consideration attributes such as shape, size, and decoration, all of which can have significant social meanings, space syntax analysis actually decreases the amount of information that can be used to understand a system.

This criticism misses the purpose of space syntax analysis, which is to focus on the elemental processes and nature of spatial arranging. Analogous to pure mathematical models, space syntax provides a compact expression of the problem—namely, the manner in which space is organized. By eliminating all extraneous variables except those that relate to the process being studied, space syntax analysis offers the clearest possible model of spatial behavior. Its simplicity and clarity facilitate the mathematical manipulation of idealized systems of nodes and linkages and provide a more understandable way to predict spatial behavior (Castri 1979:6). As two early practitioners of graph theory in the field of anthropology noted, "By representing a system of this type as a graph, one can study certain formal properties of social structure, together with their empirical implications" (Hage and Harary 1983:3).

Most spatial systems are redundant in their constituent subsystems, and the simplification of information provided by space syntax analysis enables spatial systems to be presented in less complicated and more understandable ways (Simon 1962). Few would argue that dimensional, aesthetic, visual, and acoustical properties have no meaning (Osman 1993:117), and there are architectural and cultural nuances that space syntax simply cannot reveal. This admission need not imply that space syntax has no substantial value, but it suggests the desirability of using space syntax techniques as part of a comprehensive, cross-disciplinary approach to understanding the relations between the social and the spatial.

The archaeological application of space syntax analysis can be complicated by the unavailability of descriptive material, and space syntax cannot replace information that has been lost or is otherwise unrecoverable from the archaeological record. For example, "the process of architectural deterioration...often obscures the entrances into rooms and buildings. Without precise knowledge of the location of these entrances, only a subset of the key syntactic properties can be analyzed" (Ferguson 1993:71). Fortunately, many late prehistoric structures in the Southwest, including portions of Arroyo Hondo Pueblo, retain sufficient details to permit elements such as the presence of boundaries and entrances to be teased out of the archaeological record.

Another issue concerns architectural contemporaneity in both construction and usage. A single construction episode results in a particular structural form according to the builders' design ideas (which embody social ideas). Unfortunately, archaeologists are often presented with evolved rather than designed settlements. The former type may be the consequence of particular historical contingencies and result in situations in which forms changed less than social conceptions of how those forms should be used (see, e.g., Fairclough 1992; Markus 1993; Horton 1994; Mazumdar and Mazumdar 1994). Pecos Pueblo, which was occupied for several hundred years and experienced several building episodes, is one such place.

A successful space syntax analysis requires, at a minimum, that chronological categories be sorted out, a process that should combine archaeological, historical, and ethnographic approaches. Similarly, unless one is satisfied that a series of spaces was utilized at the same time, one cannot begin to assess their topological relationships. In the Southwest and a few other areas, the availability of tree-ring dating helps to answer questions about contemporaneous construction, and archaeological excavation can often determine usage. In situations in which physical evidence of remodeling and reuse exists (Horne 1994; Lycett 1994), the problem is more manageable, but there are also situations in which reuse occurs through social action rather than by actual physical reconstruction.

Some critics (Leach 1978; Ledewitz 1991) have asserted that because Hillier and Hanson use extensive background information regarding other cultural variables that elucidate how space is utilized, they ultimately tell one nothing one does not already know. For example, in considering the relationship between depth and meaning, Stephen Ledewitz (1991:264) critiqued the possibility of always being able to read social organization from spatial organization. Depth may be used to express either the sacred or the profane (e.g., the throne room versus the privy) or may be used as means of isolating those without power (e.g., prisoners, patients, women) (Peatross 1994).

Space syntax practitioners have never denied that the availability of substantial contextual information is a necessary adjunct to analysis. Merely having an accessibility graph of a structure does not inform us about the functions of any space. If one has contextual information about the society responsible for the subject structure, it is possible at least to posit that the deepest spaces relate to the values the society assigns to the persons or things being controlled or protected. The "protected things" might include wealth, important people, sacred objects or spaces, or individual privacy. Architecture is not always uniform, and buildings can have idiosyncratic plans and styles. Before drawing conclusions about the social meanings of built spaces in a society, one should analyze a variety of vernacular and public structures in order to discover the fundamental building forms that characterize that society. Once these forms are recognized, one may go on to determine what they mean in terms of social values.

This point is cogently illustrated in a study covering several occupation periods of a Scottish castle (Fairclough 1992). Graham Fairclough was able to use historical records to provide a context for the remnant walls and doorways and demonstrate the value of a comprehensive approach to understanding the meanings behind architecture. Despite a reliance on historical records, Fairclough recognized the value of syntactic analysis for archaeology and noted: "Buildings are perhaps our principal evidence for culture and society in much of the past...and they can offer a rich source of data for social patterning and relationships. In addition, buildings are also significant because they are rarely (at least for pre-industrial periods) standardized, and they can, therefore, often bring us closer to individual decision-makers such as architects, designers and users" (Fairclough 1992:348–349).

With reference to Edlingham Castle, Fairclough found problems with the interpretation of access diagrams in terms of physical versus social use modifications. For example, some changes indicated that the "deepest" rooms were not always the "highest status" rooms, and the addition of new entries made it more difficult to understand the relationship between private and public space. Using documentary evidence to buttress his access analysis, Fairclough concluded that spatial changes were status related. If historical documents had not been available to reveal how Scottish castles became more socially stratified over time, the evidence of the additional entries (e.g., back stairs for servants) could have been erroneously interpreted as creating greater accessibility and hence less social control, when the situation was exactly the reverse. Fairclough's study nicely illustrates the importance of context in drawing behavioral inferences from syntactic analysis.

Finally, although Khaldiga Osman (1993) and Osman and Mamoun Suliman (1994, 1995, 1996) have successfully used space syntax analysis to study Sudanese houses, their critique of space syntax analysis is that it developed in the context of a western European architectural tradition, which limits its applicability to non-Western situations because of differences in the manner in which space is perceived and treated. These authors believe that Hillier and Hanson fail to account for the usage of traditional non–Western spaces such as roofs, plazas, and courtyards. As Osman described it, using the example of Sudanese houses:

> The Space Syntax Theory, as set by its authors, regards the outside node, the root, as one of the constituents of a setting. In many of the examples analyzed using this method, this node is in the front yard of a building. Consequently, it is possible that the shortest route between any two spaces may pass through an outside node. In the Sudanese context, an outside node always represents the street or the public domain; thus it is inconceivable to consider a shortest path that connects two spaces within the boundary of a building through the gate. (Osman and Suliman 1994:32)

This criticism would be significant except for the fact that space syntax analysis is sufficiently flexible to take account of different systems of syntax rules. If one is trying to analyze structures in a society in which rooftop or unbuilt open spaces play a significant role, one can account for such spaces in justified access graphs by adding one more level to the network of spaces and linkages so that the street becomes the root and plazas and rooftops are treated as part of the occupied, built space. This is the process that Orhun, Hillier, and Hanson (1995) used in their study of traditional Turkish houses, in which gardens were treated as single spaces. It is also the approach I use in the present study. When J. B. Jackson (1954:24) describes a pueblo plaza as being "more like a large room designed for some specific group function, a variation of the cell or enclosed space," he is illustrating why space syntax offers a unique opportunity to analyze Pueblo settlements. The simplicity of Pueblo design corresponds to the simplicity of space syntax. The problem raised by Osman and others illustrates why an investigator must understand the cultural context within which the analyzed space was built.

Perhaps the best approach is for archaeologists to remain cognizant of these potential problems and always be explicit about what is being analyzed. No system will ever be completely objective and error free; as one investigator suggested, "The best we can do is to arrange to be wrong about [these measurements] as consistently as possible" (Hopkins 1987:391).

ARCHAEOLOGICAL APPLICATIONS

Despite archaeologists' desire to glean the greatest amount of information from the incomplete material remains of abandoned settlements, so far the use of space syntax analysis or similar methodologies in connection with the corpus of well-preserved architectural remains has been, at best, limited. Although a number of researchers have successfully applied these techniques to a variety of archaeological sites, the majority of space syntax applications have been made in connection with either existing or historical societies for which written records were available to assist the investigators (Hillier and Hanson 1984; Hillier and Hanson 1987; Fairclough 1992; Osman and Suliman 1994; Orhun, Hillier, and Hanson 1995; Ferguson 1996, 2002; Hillier 1996). The list of archaeological applications is growing (e.g., Steadman 1996; Shapiro 1999; Bustard 2003), but what is more exciting is the discovery of cross-cultural regularities in the ways in which space is utilized. For example, several investigators have suggested that differences in integration values reflecting multiple levels of accessibility may represent some degree of social inequality (Bonanno et al. 1990b; Chapman 1990).

As one way to present the potential application of space syntax analysis, I conclude with three examples from Southwestern archaeology. Bruce Bradley (1993) used space syntax analysis to examine a series of defined "architectural suites" at Sand Canyon Pueblo in southwestern Colorado. Bradley looked at clusters of contiguous built spaces that included habitation rooms, kivas, and associated open spaces and found a strong correlation between relative accessibility values and what he called "ceremonial specialization." All suites were ostensibly arranged around kivas, but some suites had markedly lower integration values, which implied greater accessibility to adjacent public spaces, whereas other suites, with higher integration values, were presumably less well integrated and might have been domestic habitations (Bradley 1993:30). Bradley's use of space syntax analysis in concert with archaeological evidence of construction, use, and abandonment is an excellent model for the way these techniques can help provide an overall picture of settlement organization.

In addition to Cooper's work (1995), another application of space syntax to Chacoan use of space was made by Wendy Bustard (1995), who analyzed the spatial structure of a number of small-house sites.

Using accessibility graphs to calculate depth and integration values, Bustard found a consistent genotypical pattern of space usage among these sites. They were invariably arranged around a constellation of built spaces ranging from the most accessible (plazas) to the least accessible (short-term storage), with mealing spaces, as transitional areas, having intermediate integration values. This consistent spatial pattern implied a fixed pattern of social orientation that underlay the relationships within these small settlements and, according to Bustard, might have wider implications for the entire Chaco system. Unlike Cooper, who identified substantial variability among the floor plans and spatial arrangements of great houses (Cooper 1995:276), Bustard found evidence that appeared to support a lower level of behavioral ordering in which small-site residents followed an accepted convention for the arrangement and use of space.

Finally, in an ambitious study of Zuni Pueblo, T. J. Ferguson (1993, 1996, 2002) strengthened the presumption that changes in integration values imply changes in social organization. Using ethnographic and ethnohistoric sources, he delineated the links between invisible social structure and visible architectural forms. As one brief illustration, prior to the late nineteenth century the Zunis faced threats from Puebloan, Spanish, and Athapaskan groups. Although their architectural styles changed, the relatively high integration values associated with the earlier Zuni settlements did not change significantly until these external threats dissipated. A more telling point is that whereas the spatial arrangements of Zuni buildings changed over time, these changes were found to be a matter of degree rather than of kind. All three of the studies just mentioned involved different architectural styles, cultures, and issues, yet they were able to reach some unexpected conclusions through the application of a single set of analytic techniques.

5

A Space Syntax Analysis of Arroyo Hondo Pueblo

In a generalized condition of space, the sum
of all occupiable positions is the potential for creation.
—*Frederick Sommer and Stephen Aldrich,*
"The Poetic Logic of Art and Aesthetics"

Application of space syntax analysis to Arroyo Hondo Pueblo led me to three discoveries about how spatial usage changed there between the Component I and II occupations. Over time, there was an overall shift toward greater spatial segregation within roomblocks, an increased focus on plazas as primary integrating spaces, and a greater differentiation between the integration values of living rooms and storage rooms.

Space syntax analysis has its limitations, and one must be cognizant of the appropriate analytic units to be examined. Roomblocks and groups of contiguous rooms within partial roomblocks are useful analytic units for understanding the underlying structures of ancestral Pueblo architecture. In space syntax terms, the analysis of individual roomblocks is akin to looking at access patterns in a series of large houses, and the focus is on learning how people moved through and experienced those spaces.

Selecting entities that are both useful and appropriate for analysis is only the first step. In chapter 3 I considered questions about room usage and abandonment and their relationship to effective syntactic analysis. In this chapter I continue in that vein by describing the logic of movement among rooms and plazas.

UNITS OF ANALYSIS AND INFERENCES ABOUT MOVEMENT

Prior studies of Arroyo Hondo's architecture identified residence units of different sizes on the basis of doorway locations within roomblocks (Beal 1972; Creamer 1993). In describing these units, Winifred Creamer assumed that all doorways were open contemporaneously (Creamer 1993:122), an assumption I adopted for the present study. Although the identification of residence units can be helpful, such units are not necessarily coincident with mapped accessibility routes, in which topological rather than familial relationships among spaces are stressed. One problem with delineating "residence units" or "households" in terms of access analysis is that the ways in which pueblo spaces were connected means that some movements were more likely than others.

Consider the problem of determining movement between single-room residence units. A number of these units have been identified at Arroyo Hondo, and their existence is further supported by ethnographic evidence such as that collected by Victor Mindeleff among the Hopis (1891:101) and by observations made at Santa Clara Pueblo (Hill 1982:74). For the Component II occupation, the majority of rooms had no doorways to indicate interroom connections, but Creamer (1993:130) made the working assumption that two rooms—a living room and a storage room—composed a residence unit. Inferences regarding residence units are important, but they do not necessarily resolve questions about intraroomblock access. The problem can be illustrated by considering potential movement through roomblock 16 during Component II times. As will be seen later in figure 5.12, the series of interior residential rooms in this roomblock must have had some access to plaza C. In the absence of doorways, access must have been via rooftops. The question then becomes, Which roofs could one cross? The issue is further complicated by the archaeological fact that not all rooftops reveal evidence of domestic use; one might assume that some rooftops were more likely to have been used as transitional spaces than others.

60

Using ethnographic analogy, the question can be posed whether rooftops at Arroyo Hondo were akin to the roofs used as public walkways that A. L. Kroeber noted at Zuni Pueblo (Kroeber 1917:189) or to the roofs used as individual front yards that Mindeleff found among the Hopis (Mindeleff 1891:151). Using historical maps and photographs of Zuni Pueblo, Karen Dohm (1996:89) tested Kroeber's view and concluded that "architecturally, the roofs are more or less private and the way rooftops are used is more or less private". However, a variety of historical photographs taken on ceremonial occasions suggest that at least some roofs at Zuni were sometimes used as public or quasi-public spaces, suggesting a multiplicity of uses that may not be reducible to an either-or situation.

In addition to observing the use of rooftops as "yards," Mindeleff noted other kinds of uses for them at Hopi that suggested potential impediments to unrestricted walking:

> Even their [first-floor room] roofs are largely utilized for the temporary storage of many household articles, and in the autumn, after the harvests have been gathered, the terraces and copings are often covered with drying peaches, and the peculiar long strips into which pumpkins and squash have been cut to facilitate their desiccation for winter use. Among other things the household supply of wood is sometimes piled up at one end of this terrace, but more commonly the natives have so many other uses for this space that the sticks of fuel are piled up on a rude projecting skeleton of poles, supported on one side by two upright forked sticks set into the ground, and on the other resting upon the stone coping of the wall. (Mindeleff 1891:103; see also Dohm 1996:89–90)

Unfortunately, the archaeological record is insufficiently complete to provide evidence of all the foregoing kinds of activities. One assumption made for this study was that rooftop movement at Arroyo Hondo was not completely random and unrestricted but followed a "shortest route" pattern. For example, evidence of doorways between first-floor rooms implies that movement took place between them, and I assumed that rooftop movement followed the same pattern. This assumption is illustrated in figure 5.1. In fact, people might have walked across more roofs than merely those of underlying houses with interconnecting doorways, and there is no unequivocal way to prove that the set of "shortest direct routes" was the only set of pathways. On the

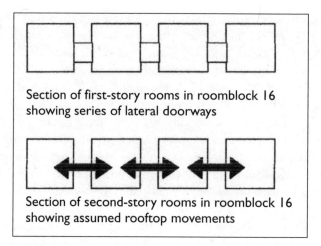

Figure 5.1. Assumed pattern of rooftop movement in relation to doorways for Arroyo Hondo Pueblo.

other hand, this approach permits one to take rooftop spaces into account and provides an element of uniformity in the analysis because it has a logical consistency with the internal spaces whose access relationships are relatively clear.

Wall vents were another class of architectural feature that I considered in identifying potential pathways (fig. 5.2). Vents, which were neither rare nor ubiquitous in either component, were circular or oval holes used for ventilation or communication (see Creamer 1993: 113–116). Component I vents ranged from 9 to 41 centimeters in diameter and were bimodally distributed, being situated either more than 1 meter or fewer than 25 centimeters above the floor (Creamer 1993:33). Component II vents were more uniform in size, averaging 9–10 centimeters in diameter, but were located anywhere from 42 centimeters above the floor to actual floor level (Creamer 1993:50).

Archaeological evidence of wall vents between two rooms suggested some kind of association between those rooms, so I deemed movement across the roofs of vent-linked rooms more likely than not. The argument is that the presence of vents means that the communication of sights, sounds, and smells was less restricted between vent-connected rooms than between rooms lacking vents. This potential for communication between rooms suggested the kinds of domestic relationships that would facilitate rooftop travel without regard to claims of "private" rooftop space.

Figure 5.2. Arroyo Hondo pueblo roomblock excavations showing vent holes (photograph by David Grant Noble, School of American Research Arroyo Hondo Collections).

The existence of rooftop activity areas may also relate to the issue of movement, in that they might be viewed as extensions of underlying private domestic spaces. In defining such spaces archaeologically, Creamer relied on previous work by Jeffrey S. Dean (1996), who used evidence of firepits or hearths, mealing bins and metates, and large holes for storage or grinding as defining attributes for activity areas (Creamer 1993:111). In the case of Arroyo Hondo, this functional category was based on the presence of ground stone tools and hearths in roof-fall strata (Creamer 1993:119).

Table 5.1 summarizes the available information about rooftop activity areas and vents for all excavated areas at Arroyo Hondo Pueblo. I suggest that the presence of both features strongly indicates linkages between the involved rooms. This view is supported by ethnographic descriptions of the manner in which rooms were added onto existing residences in the Hopi villages in order to accommodate growing households or married children (Mindeleff 1891:102).

With respect to rooms entered directly from plazas, there is some archaeological evidence of ladder impressions at Arroyo Hondo, and I assumed that ladder access to rooftops existed at those points. In addition, I assumed that any room bordering directly on a plaza and identified by an earlier researcher as a living room probably had direct

TABLE 5.1

Correlation of Rooftop Activity Areas and Vent Holes
for Arroyo Hondo Pueblo

Component	Excavated (Total) Rooms	Rooftop Activity Areas	Vent Holes	Rooftop Activity Areas and Vents
I	100 (1,000)	21	17	1
II	50 (200)	14	15	6
Roomblock 16, CI	19 (64)	4	4	0
Roomblock 16, CII	22 (42)	5	5	4

Source: Adapted from Creamer 1993.

ladder access from the plaza through a rooftop hatchway. Where a two-story unit with no apparent first-floor entry bordered directly on a plaza, I concluded that access to the second-floor roof entry was from an adjacent first-story roof.

Plazas have been incorporated into space syntax analyses cross-culturally because they represent more than mere open space (Iowa 1985; Swentzell 1988, 1992; Osman and Suliman 1994, 1995). Although most often considered to be places where recurrent, highly visible, community-wide rituals take place (Moore 1996:140), they are also sites of many more prosaic activities. The functional attributes of plazas have been considered by a number of authors, some of whom have drawn comparisons between European and Native American plazas (Swentzell 1988, 1992; Anella 1992; Low 1995). The operative principle appears to be that Pueblo plazas are somehow more "human-centered" and open to the world at large than are centrifugally oriented European plazas, which are designed to pull, hold, and control people (Anella 1992:40–41).

Inasmuch as every culture interprets and transforms the landscape in ways that reinforce and are consistent with its worldview (Basso 1996), one can argue that Pueblo plazas are every bit as controlling of individual behavior as European plazas but that the cultural ideals are different. Pueblo plazas are accessible to many people and are constructed to facilitate group solidarity in situations of diverse and competing interests (fig. 5.3). The idea of "cooperation," which underlies

Figure 5.3. View of Taos Pueblo plaza (courtesy of Jason S. Shapiro).

much of what has been written about ancestral Pueblo society,
becomes an offshoot of the combined self-interests of all the residents
of a village. Mary Douglas (1991:299) wrote about the balancing of
individual needs and the "public good" in what she called "visual communities": "The theoretical solution…is fairness, but the practical solution is to make every member a watchdog on the public behalf and to
use coordination to do the rest. Coordination facilitates public moni-
toring and a high degree of visibility."

All comings and goings, as well as other activities, are visible within a Pueblo plaza, and the integration values of plazas at Arroyo Hondo,
particularly during Component II, are relatively low, implying that they
were highly integrating spaces. Nothing that occurs in a plaza goes
unnoticed, at least by residents of the immediately surrounding roomblocks, and the presence of new activities or strangers is immediately
discovered. Far from being a no-man's-land, the plaza is the ultimate
example of a controlled environment in which mutual observation
forces people to conform to patterns of behavior that accord with
group norms. A study by Wesley Bernardini (1996) suggests that the
architectural convention of the plaza is a manifestation of social forces
directed toward alleviating organizational stress through the control of
public rituals. This theme is consistent with the results of space syntax

65

Figure 5.4. View of excavated Plaza G, Arroyo Hondo (photograph by David Grant Noble, School of American Research Arroyo Hondo Collections).

analysis except that it artificially narrows the multifaceted roles of plazas, which influence social behavior during nonritual as well as ritual events.

The plazas associated with both occupations at Arroyo Hondo were used intensively, and any doubt about the efficacy of including plazas within the ambit of "built space" for syntactic analysis should be eliminated in light of the archaeological evidence (fig. 5.4). "Numerous features indicate that a variety of domestic activities took place in plazas, features included mealing areas, ovens, turkey pens, basins, dividing walls, ramadas or portales, and numerous burials.... Use of plazas for religious activities is indicated by the location of kivas in several of these open areas" (Creamer 1993:57).

The incorporation of plazas into the space syntax calculations for Arroyo Hondo does not imply a lack of awareness of the important differences between rooms and plazas. One might question the treatment of plazas as single, unified built spaces, because some evidence suggests the existence of demarcated subdivisions within some plazas (Creamer 1993:72–73) and because not all of the previously listed activities occurred in random patterns. Some activities, such as burial and food preparation, undoubtedly had spatial components and were

Figure 5.5. View of partially excavated roomblock 16 (photograph by David Grant Noble, School of American Research Arroyo Hondo Collections).

performed in the vicinity of roomblocks (Creamer 1993:70, 76, 82, 87), whereas other kinds of work were carried out in a variety of plaza locations. The presence and use of kivas also served to delineate plaza space. For the present analysis, however, the archaeological evidence was insufficiently fine-grained to justify any spatial subdivision within plazas, so I treated them as single, indivisible spatial units.

The issue of room function is also worthy of some clarification. Creamer (1993:113–116, 165–207) used eight functional room categories: storage, living, living or storage (precise use indeterminate), ceremonial, ceremonial storage, other functions (unspecified), and function indeterminate. She categorized rooms largely on the basis of excavated intramural features and material remains in a manner consistent with prior studies in Southwestern archaeology (Hill 1970; Adams 1989; Creamer 1993:110; Dean 1996). For example, she identified rooms as living rooms if they contained a hearth, two or more wall entries, and internal features such as niches, vents, peg holes, and shelves. It was never my purpose to reevaluate Creamer's detailed analyses; I incorporated her functional categories directly into my space syntax analysis. A summary of the functions associated with excavated rooms is included in Appendix A.

Although the two components at Arroyo Hondo shared a basic

67

material culture as well as architectural forms, there are clear differences in the manner in which space was arranged during the two occupations (fig. 5.5). What follows is an application of space syntax analysis to three excavated roomblocks from each component that reveals the basis for this statement.[1]

COMPONENT I

Roomblock 16

The single most completely excavated roomblock at Arroyo Hondo was roomblock 16, which appears to have been built initially as a Component I roomblock and then rebuilt during Component II. Figure 5.6 is a detailed diagram of the Component I portions of roomblock 16, showing the relationships among its built spaces. Altogether, 15 numbered rooms were thoroughly excavated on this level (out of approximately 68–69 identified rooms), and some information, such as the presence of doorways, is known for several adjacent rooms that were not otherwise excavated.[2]

Irrespective of the existence of interconnecting doorways between several first-floor rooms, there were none among the second-story rooms. Creamer suggested that doorways "presumably" connected interior and exterior second-story spaces (Creamer 1993:22), but the excavation data revealed no such evidence. In his report on the excavations at the late-fourteenth-century site of Poshuouinge, J. A. Jeançon (1923:13–14) opined that "it must be remembered that only the lower walls are now standing and that the upper stories probably had doorways leading out onto the terraces that were formed by the lower rooms." In light of the analogous conditions at Arroyo Hondo, the absence of evidence for second-story doorways is not surprising, but the space syntax analysis proceeded on the rebuttable presumption that such doorways did not exist and that entry into second-story rooms was through floor and ceiling hatchways. Creamer identified all the second-floor rooms as living rooms, a conclusion supported by archaeological evidence and ethnographic information (Morgan 1881; Mindeleff 1891).

Most of the first-floor rooms were identified as general storage rooms. The exception was room 33, identified as a ceremonial storage room that formed a two-story unit with the ceremonial room above it (room 33a; Creamer 1993:117). This identification is important for

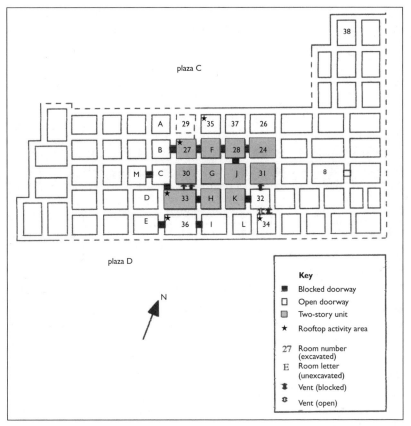

Figure 5.6. Schematic plan of roomblock 16, Component I. Adapted from Creamer 1993:113–114, 178–183.

inferring access, because it suggests that rooms 33 and 33a occupied a relatively central position in the roomblock, so movement was toward room 33 as a destination from adjacent spaces rather than the room's having been a transitional space used as a passage to another room.

In order to travel, hypothetically, from the front of roomblock 16 (the row of rooms adjacent to plaza C) to the rear (the row of rooms adjacent to plaza D), people would, I assumed, go around, as opposed to up and over, the central group of two-story rooms. Aside from such a route's being literally the path of least resistance, there were more lateral than front-to-back openings through this section. In addition, there were few clearly defined rooftop activity areas to interfere with

69

such movement. In these respects, Component I was very different from Component II, when both front–to–back connections and rooftop activity areas were more prevalent.

Figure 5.7 is a justified access graph of a portion of roomblock 16.[3] Although the roomblock was bordered by the "open spaces" of plazas C and D, the analytical perspective is from the carrier space, that undifferentiated zone located beyond the plazas. This graph is not offered as the only possible set of connections and circuits but represents a reasonable fit between potential access routes and the locations of the roomblock spaces. The syntactic pattern of roomblock 16 is essentially symmetrical and distributed, meaning that there is a relatively high degree of accessibility among its spaces (see chapter 3). This spatial pattern has been associated with less hierarchical forms of social organization. In the case of Arroyo Hondo, these findings are consistent with relatively egalitarian tribal models such as those suggested by Ann Palkovich (1980) and Judith Habicht-Mauche (1993). Although it would be appropriate to discuss the spatial attributes of tribal models, no such analyses presently exist. Such a lacuna does not invalidate Palkovich's or Habicht-Mauche's interpretation but merely raises the possibility of additional testable hypotheses. For the entire roomblock 16 sample, the mean integration value is 1.01, which is at the borderline of values that distinguish integrated from segregated spaces (Hillier and Hanson 1984:113).[4]

Aside from its larger size, the Component I layout of roomblock 16 is distinguished from that of Component II by the presence of lateral doorways. Laurel Cooper (1995) commented about lateral doorways in her analysis of Chacoan great houses and observed that such features permit a substantial amount of depth to develop in relatively limited areas. Despite the number of connections, the depth of such structures may actually create somewhat higher integration values. This seems to be the case in roomblock 16, where, despite numerous doorways, overall depth seems to have contributed to the integration value of 1.01. In virtually all cases, the deepest and most controlled rooms are first-story storage areas located toward the middle of the roomblock. The shallowest and most accessible spaces are a few first- and second-story residential units (see fig. 5.7, rooms C, G, H), rather than the plazas, a finding that is somewhat inconsistent with the traditional role assigned to plazas as integrating spaces (Swentzell 1988, 1992; Anella 1992). These findings are explained by the fact that integration values

70

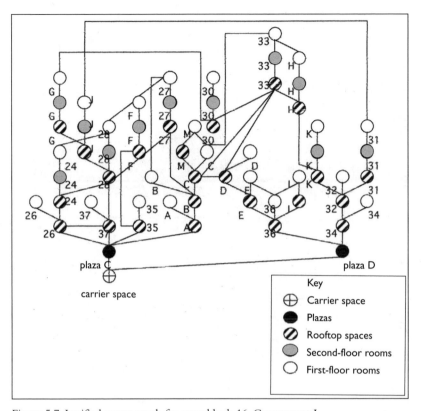

Figure 5.7. Justified access graph for roomblock 16, Component I.

are based on the connections rather than merely the locations of selected spaces. Spaces that can be accessed via multiple pathways always
have lower values than spaces having fewer such connections.

   With regard to localized measures, the rooftop spaces for rooms 32
and D had the highest control values, indicating that they maintained
the greatest degree of local control over adjacent spaces (see Appendix
A). Plaza C, which is far from the most integrated space relative to the
entire roomblock, exhibited the fourth highest control value, meaning
that it was still a powerful local space. The rooms with the lowest control values in roomblock 16 were all first-floor rooms with no connections to other rooms except for the second-floor rooms immediately
above them. This means that the most highly integrated and the most
controlling spaces are not necessarily the same, implying a differentiation of functions. By the same token, the deepest and most controlled

71

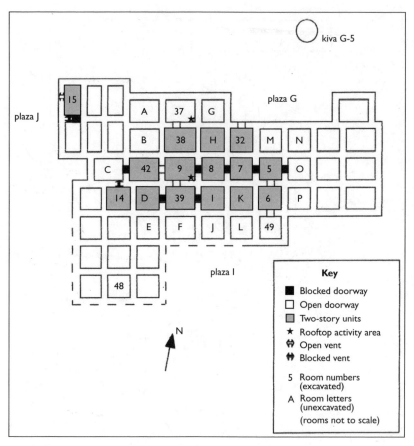

Figure 5.8. Schematic plan of roomblock 18, Component I. Adapted from Creamer 1993:114, 127.

rooms are not always the same as the rooms that exercise the weakest control in the system.

Roomblock 18

In many respects, the results of the analysis of roomblock 18, shown in figure 5.8, were very similar to those for roomblock 16. Fourteen first-floor and 10 second-floor rooms were excavated, out of approximately 52 rooms associated with this roomblock. As in roomblock 16, all the second-story rooms were identified as living rooms and the first-floor rooms as storage rooms.

Within this roomblock were a number of second-story spaces that formed a dominant group along the middle of the long axis of the roomblock. Room 32 was a two-story unit that contained one of the few first-floor openings onto a plaza (Creamer 1993:126). Because of this opening, coupled with the presence of kiva G-5, it initially appeared that movement into this roomblock was oriented primarily through plaza G. Yet it seems reasonable to assume that some access to the roomblock was available through plaza I, despite the lack of extensive excavation there. Figure 5.9, the justified access graph, therefore shows connections from both plazas.

As in roomblock 16, living and storage spaces were linked by relatively complex connections in a series of deep circuits. In terms of movement within roomblock 18, there were numerous interior doorways, the majority of them (8 out of 14) being lateral connections. One series of doorways (all but one of which were found blocked) even linked seven rooms in a line (O, 5, 7, 8, 9, 42, C). If all these doorways had been open at some time, they would have connected at least a dozen ground-floor rooms. Fewer vents and rooftop activity areas were identified for roomblock 18 than for roomblock 16, but overall the nature of the room arrangements and manner of access appeared quite similar in the two.

The average integration value for roomblock 18 is 1.07, only slightly higher than the value obtained for roomblock 16. Although a visual examination of the spatial arrangement of roomblock 18 suggests a more permeable structure—one that was relatively easy to move through—the integration value suggests a system operating at the upper end of those that have been labeled "integrated." Despite its myriad circuits and lateral connections, this roomblock consists of spaces that are not particularly well integrated. As in roomblock 16, the existence of alternative access paths (which contribute to lower integration values) is outweighed by the depth of those pathways within the roomblock, which makes rooms relatively difficult to reach from the outside and contributes to the higher integration value.

With reference to control values, roomblock 18 shows at least one major difference from roomblock 16, namely, that plaza G had by far the highest value and exercised the greatest control over other spaces. Although a number of rooftop spaces have control values in excess of 1.00 (see Appendix A), the differences between these values and that for plaza G are much greater than the range of values calculated for roomblock 16. As in roomblock 16, however, the weakest spaces in

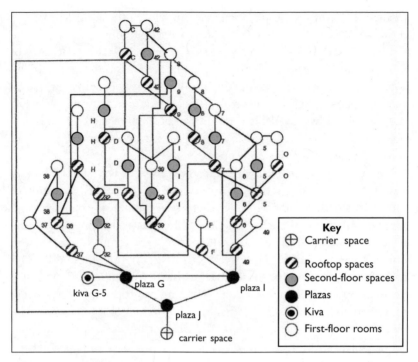

Figure 5.9. Justified access graph for roomblock 18, Component I.

terms of control are first-floor rooms with only a single connection each to a neighboring space. The overall closeness in integration value to that obtained for roomblock 16 implies a consistent pattern of space usage, an implication that is further strengthened by an examination of roomblocks 5 and 6.

Roomblocks 5 and 6

Consistent with prior studies of Arroyo Hondo (Creamer 1993:124–126), roomblocks 5 and 6 were treated as a single entity. These adjacent roomblocks, shown in figure 5.10, are unusual because they protrude like a peninsula from the northern edge of the pueblo and do not fully enclose a plaza. Instead, they are bordered by two poorly defined plazas (plaza L on the west and plaza K on the east) that constituted potential access points into these roomblocks. I treated these two plazas as separate spaces for the purposes of space syntax

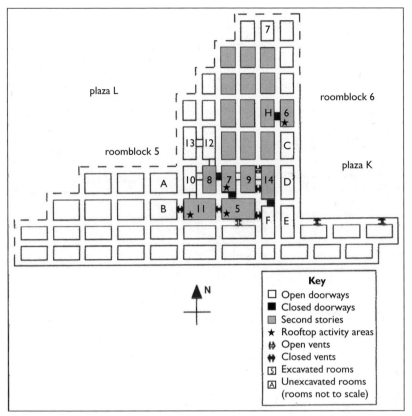

Figure 5.10. Schematic plan of roomblock 5–6, Component I. Adapted from Creamer 1993:113, 127.

analysis. Eleven first-story and seven second-story rooms were excavated in this roomblock, and although evidence for 10 doorways was recorded, the unusual orientation of this section of the pueblo makes it difficult to describe them as being either lateral or front-to-back. As can be seen in figure 5.10, 6 of the 10 doorways connect through the longer axes of the rooms, as in front-to-back connections, and run perpendicular to the long axis of the entire roomblock. The remaining four doorways connect across short axes, as in lateral connections, and run parallel to the axis of the roomblock.

As in roomblocks 16 and 18, the central core of roomblock 5–6 had a series of two-story spaces surrounded by one-story rooms. In

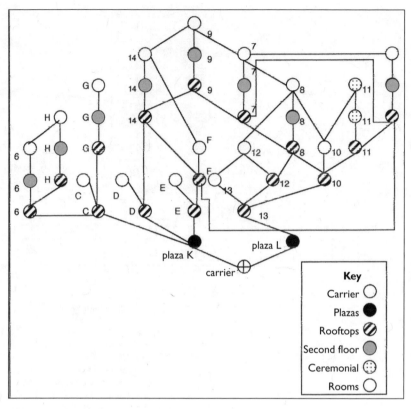

Figure 5.11. Justified access graph for roomblock 5–6, Component I.

addition, nine of the doorways in roomblock 5–6 form a potential labyrinth that could have connected approximately 16 first- and second-story rooms, a degree of circuitry that seems to typify Component I roomblocks.

Figure 5.11 is the justified access graph for the connections between the rooms. The average integration value is 1.03, similar to those calculated for the other Component I roomblocks. The dual access from plazas K and L, together with the combination of lateral and axial doorways, created a number of alternative paths within the roomblock. The depth of these circuits was the most likely reason the average integration value was not lower, simply because it was still relatively difficult to access these rooms deep within the block.

The control values follow the general pattern seen in the previous two roomblocks. The rooftop of a two-story interior room (room 14) has the highest value, and first-story rooms that are somewhat peripheral to the section being analyzed (rooms A and C) have the lowest values. The plazas show mixed results, with plaza K in excess of 1.00 (1.667), indicating a large degree of control, and plaza L having a value below 1.00 (0.583), indicating a small degree of control. Part of this discrepancy is undoubtedly due to the availability of archaeological data, because no excavations were conducted in either plaza.

Integration Values Associated with Component I Room Functions

· When the mean integration values associated with Component I rooms having defined functions in roomblocks 16, 18, and 5–6 are compared, an interesting pattern can be seen. Table 5.2 shows the mean values for six categories of rooms, calculated from the information in Appendix A. Storage spaces have a slightly higher integration value than do living spaces, and spaces that were originally living rooms but were subsequently converted to storage have a value almost intermediate between those of the two classes. (Of course, not every living room had a lower integration value than every storage room, and not every converted room had an intermediate integration value.)

The explanation for this pattern is not immediately clear but may relate to the facts that storage spaces consistently lie "deeper" within the network than living spaces; the change always appears to have been from living to storage and not vice versa; and there is some evidence that construction of second-story rooms resulted in the transformation of some first-floor living spaces into storage spaces (Beal 1972:90). This last occurrence would have created slightly deeper and more segregated spaces—not as segregated as planned storage spaces but less accessible than living spaces.

Component I ceremonial spaces exhibited the lowest mean integration value—that is, they were the most highly integrated of all the room types—consistent with their presumed role as spaces of social integration. In contrast, their associated storage rooms had the highest—most segregated—value. This apparent dichotomy suggests that whereas the accessibility of ceremonial rooms encouraged entry for specific ceremonies, people were generally discouraged from entering ceremonial storage rooms, to which access presumably was controlled by select individuals.

The analysis of Component I rooms reveals a combination of

TABLE *5.2*

Mean Integration Values by Room Function for Component I
Roomblocks 16, 18, and 5–6 ($n = 59$)

Room Function	Mean Integration Value
Storage ($n = 16$)	1.12
Living ($n = 22$)	1.07
Living converted to storage ($n = 13$)	1.09
Living or storage (undetermined) ($n = 3$)	1.11
Ceremonial ($n = 3$)	1.01
Ceremonial storage ($n = 2$)	1.18

Note: Rooms labeled "O" for "other function" or "NF" for "function indeterminate"
were not included in these calculations. The classification "ceremonial" includes values associated with kiva G-5, accessed from roomblock 18.

patterns. There is a general progression of integration values (lower values meaning greater potential accessibility and less potential control;
higher values meaning less potential accessibility and greater potential
control) that reveals ceremonial rooms to have been the most highly
integrated spaces. Living rooms were generally more integrated than
storage rooms, and ceremonial storage rooms were the least integrated
spaces of all. Irrespective of whether these findings are surprising to
anyone familiar with the archaeology of ancestral Puebloan settlements, space syntax analysis supports them with numerical values. The
general patterns identified for Component I are not only consistent but
become more pronounced in Component II.

COMPONENT II

Component II, consisting of approximately 200 rooms, was a
much less extensive settlement than Component I. Its smaller size,
together with its complete absence of two-story structures, made the
application of space syntax analysis somewhat less complicated than it
was for the earlier component.

Roomblock 16

Component II roomblock 16 was built on the ruins of the earlier

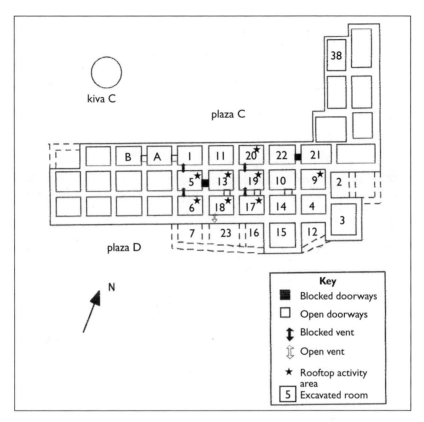

Figure 5.12. Schematic plan of roomblock 16, Component II. Adapted from Creamer 1993:129.

roomblock. Figure 5.12 shows the arrangement of the Component II rooms. A row identified mostly as living rooms (rooms 1, 11, 20, 21) fronts plaza C, and a row of mostly storage rooms occupies the middle of the block.[5] Directly south of the storage rooms is a second row of living rooms that in three adjacent cases (rooms 14, 17, and 18) had open doorways into the storage rooms. These pairs of rooms were identified as two-room residences. The functional situation was complicated by the finding that three of the rooms classified as living rooms in the southern row had sealed hearths, raising the possibility of alternative functions. To the south of this second row of living rooms, fronting plaza D, was a series of utility rooms, miscellaneous use areas, and trash disposal spaces.

None of the rooms bordering plazas C or D had doorways opening onto the plazas, so they were most likely entered via ladders and ceiling hatchways (Creamer 1993:47). Although the portion of plaza C immediately adjacent to roomblock 16 was not excavated, several ladder rests were identified from areas in plaza C adjacent to roomblocks 10 and 11, as well as in several Component II rooms, including room 16-5 (Creamer 1993:48, 81–82). I presume that similar ladder rests were located in the vicinity of roomblock 16 and gave access to ceiling entries in the first row of living rooms. Because all Component II rooms were single-story and plaza C was the only enclosed Component II plaza (plazas D and F were apparently used during the Component II occupancy but were not enclosed), Creamer believed that all the rooms were oriented toward plaza C in a front-to-back alignment.

This assertion is supported by the fact that three of five interior doorways and all seven vents were oriented in the same north-south direction. Additional support is provided by considering the area to the north of plaza D (rooms 7, 12, 15, 16, 23) that was used for trash dumping rather than for residence or storage. It seems likely that refuse-related activities took place behind rather than in front of residences. Finally, there have been a number of ethnographic observations of front-to-back room arrangements in Pueblo residence units (Mindeleff 1891:223; Nabokov and Easton 1989:371; Lycett 1994:13).

With respect to the relationships among the excavated rooms in Component II roomblock 16, Creamer (1993:126, 128) suggested, primarily on the basis of the doorways between the rooms, that there were five one-room residential units, three two-room units, and one three-room unit. Irrespective of whether these rooms actually functioned as units, the doorways clearly suggest a series of paths through the roomblock. Consistent with the treatment of Component I roomblocks, however, and for the purpose of syntactic analysis, the absence of doorways did not entirely preclude the possibility that certain rooms were on the same pathway.

The alignment of the justified access graph for the excavated portions of roomblock 16 (fig. 5.13) is consistent with the information already mentioned suggesting that the roomblock was oriented toward plaza C. The individual elements variously exhibit all four qualities— symmetry and asymmetry, distributedness and nondistributedness—but the overall impression is that of a fundamentally symmetrical and nondistributed system.

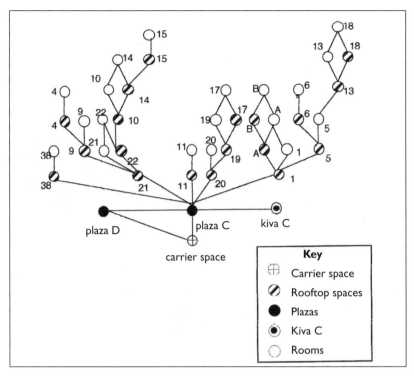

Figure 5.13. Justified access graph for roomblock 16, Component II.

For the most part, room arrangements are branched and candelabra-like, and although there are five simple loops, the observed circuitry is much less extensive than it was in the Component I roomblocks. This type of symmetrical and nondistributed arrangement suggests more social segregation during Component II than during Component I. The average integration value of 1.39 supports this conclusion. This value is much higher than those for the Component I roomblocks, implying a fundamental difference in the way in which space was arranged. In general, access to individual spaces within the roomblock was more easily controlled, or, to put it differently, more privacy was maintained, particularly among the deeper spaces.

The control values also show a different pattern, with plaza C having a substantially higher value (4.08) than any other space in the roomblock. The presence of the kiva in plaza C contributed heavily to this control value, but even if the kiva space is discounted, the plaza's

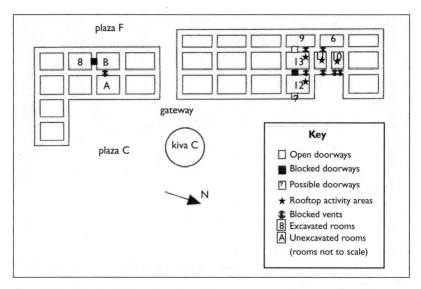

Figure 5.14. Schematic plan of roomblock 9, Component II. Adapted from Creamer 1993:129.

control value remains substantially higher than those of the other spaces. The least controlling space is actually the kiva itself, because it can be accessed through only one other space, the plaza. These data suggest a change in the use of plaza space for Component II. Plazas became much more important, with plaza C having both the lowest integration value (that is, being the most connected space) and the highest control value (being the most controlling space) within the entire roomblock. A more detailed discussion of the significance of this finding, and of the fact that all three of the Component II roomblocks analyzed had higher integration values and different patterns of control values than Component I roomblocks, is provided in chapter 7.

Roomblock 9

Roomblock 9 was excavated less extensively than roomblock 16, but I judged it to have provided enough architectural information to enable a reasonable comparison with the other roomblocks. Seven of approximately 28 rooms in the block were excavated (fig. 5.14), and of these seven, four were identified as living rooms and three as storage rooms.[6]

Consistent with the information for Component II roomblock 16,

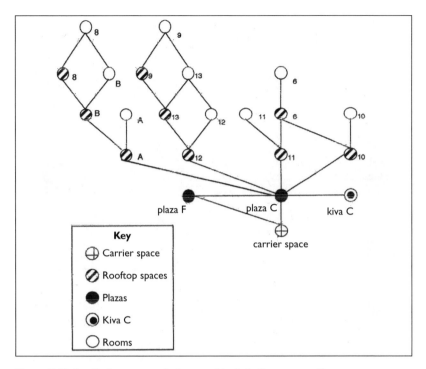

Figure 5.15. Justified access graph for roomblock 9, Component II.

a front-to-back arrangement apparently obtained in roomblock 9, with the rooms oriented east-west toward plaza C. In addition to the placement of doorways, which supports the inference of a front-to-back arrangement, all seven of the vents discovered in this roomblock had the same orientation. Wall vents may be less persuasive than doorways for inferring connections between rooms, but to the extent that they can be interpreted in this way, the seven subject spaces were likely on the same access path.

In the justified access graph for the excavated portions of roomblock 9 (fig. 5.15), we see some of the same branching and looping that was observed in roomblock 16, but the analyzed area is smaller and, in some respects, less complex in terms of numbers of branches and circuitry. The overall impression is that of a fundamentally symmetrical and nondistributed system. The average integration value for this roomblock, 1.22, is slightly lower than that for roomblock 16 but is still greater than the values for any of the Component I rooms. It lends support to the finding that space usage during Component II was different from that during Component I.

The most integrated space is plaza C, which also has the highest control number. Without repeating the comments made in connection with roomblock 16, it is apparent that the overall relationships among the Component II spaces in roomblock 9 reflect a more segregated spatial system than that seen during Component I. Traversing roomblock 9 might not have required navigating as many nodes as in a Component I roomblock, but once a particular destination was selected, far fewer alternative pathways were available to get there. Even getting into the roomblock required traversing the plaza, the most controlling space of all.

Roomblock 10

Roomblock 10 provided the smallest group of excavated Component II rooms in the study (4 out of approximately 21 rooms in the block), but it still offered sufficient information for analysis (fig. 5.16). Even with such a small number of potential nodes (two unexcavated rooms were included because of their probable association with the excavated units), the same patterns discovered for roomblocks 16 and 9 appear to hold. Although there were two doorways with lateral, east–west connections from room 6, there were also three vents in the room that suggested a front-to-back orientation toward plaza C. Consistent with other Component II findings, these vents appeared in rooms with rooftop activity areas. Access to this small group of rooms was via room 6, which had a variety of architectural features and appeared to connect to the other spaces in this group.

In some respects, the branching patterns shown in the justified access graph for roomblock 10 (fig. 5.17) are reminiscent of those in roomblocks 16 and 9, and there were no discernible circuits. In light of the branching form, it is not surprising that roomblock 10 had a relatively high mean integration value, 1.29. Consistent with its multiple doorways and central position, the rooftop space above room 6 had the lowest integration value; plaza C had the second lowest. Also consistent with roomblocks 16 and 9, plaza C exhibited the highest control value in connection with roomblock 10. Overall, roomblock 10 follows the Component II pattern of relatively segregated spaces and provides more evidence to support the assertion that some form of spatial

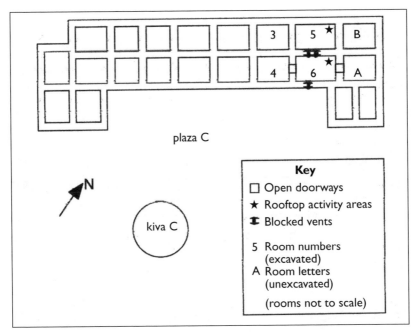

Figure 5.16. Schematic plan of roomblock 10, Component II. Adapted from Creamer 1993:130.

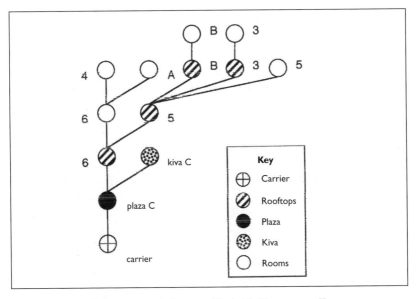

Figure 5.17. Justified access graph for roomblock 10, Component II.

TABLE 5.3

Mean Integration Values by Room Function for Component II
Roomblocks 16, 9, and 10 ($n = 30$)

Room Function	Mean Integration Value
Storage ($n = 7$)	1.65
Living ($n = 17$)	1.41
Living or storage ($n = 3$)	1.45
Ceremonial ($n = 3$)	1.03

Note: The only ceremonial room in Component II was kiva C, which, despite being potentially accessible from three different roomblocks (accounting for the figure $n = 3$), was probably subjected to restricted entry in some undetermined manner.

separation correlates with the temporal separation between the two occupations at Arroyo Hondo.

Integration Values Associated with Component II Room Functions

As in the case of Component I, a pattern of integration values was associated with specific classes of Component II rooms. Table 5.3 shows the mean integration values for four classes of rooms.[7] In comparison with the Component I values (see table 5.2), the values for storage and living rooms are more widely separated. As in Component I, not all of the individual room values follow this pattern precisely, but the overall inference of differences in the nature of room function— that is, space usage—is strengthened. For reasons explained in the following chapter, the overall trend was to place storage rooms deeper inside the system.

SUMMARY

Table 5.4 summarizes several calculated values for Components I and II. The data are displayed graphically in the box plots in figures 5.18 and 5.19. As revealed in these figures, the integration values associated with Component I structures were consistently lower than those associated with Component II structures. Although all of the roomblocks represent relatively segregated spatial arrangements, there was a significant trend over time toward even greater segregation. Statistical comparison of the integration values of Components I and II using the

TABLE 5.4

Summary of Integration Values for Arroyo Hondo Components I and II

Roomblock and Component	No. Spaces	No. Links	Mean Integration Value	Node with Lowest Value	Node with Highest Value	High-Low Difference
16, I	62	84	1.01	0.68	1.23	0.55
18, I	64	84	1.07	0.66	1.68	1.02
5–6, I	44	64	1.03	0.68	1.58	0.89
16, II	42	47	1.39	0.71	2.21	1.50
9, II	20	22	1.22	0.51	1.84	1.33
10, II	15	16	1.29	0.49	1.78	1.29

Student's T-test at the 95 percent level of confidence indicated that the components represent statistically separate populations. In addition, the range between the highest and lowest integration values for individual rooms in a roomblock increased between Components I and II.

The increased differences between high and low values in the Component II roomblocks suggest greater separation between what might be called private and public functions. This observation is noteworthy when one considers that plazas became the most integrating spaces during Component II. There is no question that plazas were extremely important during Component I as well, but they became more central to residents of Arroyo Hondo Pueblo during Component II. This trend was consistent throughout the Component II site; in two of the three roomblocks analyzed (16 and 9), the plaza exhibited the single most integrating value. Considering the small number of excavated spaces in roomblock 10, it is possible that additional information would reveal the bordering plaza to have been its most integrating space as well. In none of the three Component I roomblocks was a plaza found to be the most integrating space. Instead, each of these three had as its most integrating space one of several second-story rooftops located above a habitation room in the interior portion of the roomblock.[8] What all this suggests is a system in which individual dwellings were designed to retain a modicum of independence within a common spatial hierarchy.

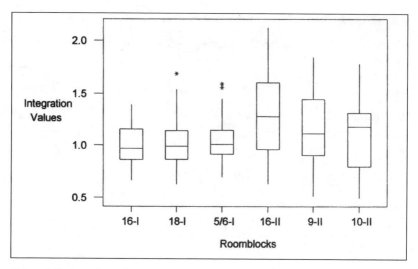

Figure 5.18. Box plots of mean integration values for individual roomblocks, Components I and II.

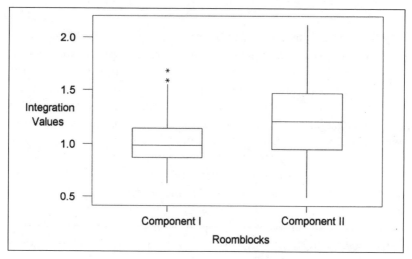

Figure 5.19. Box plots of mean integration values for Components I and II.

Another pattern that emerged from the analysis was that of increasing differentiation between functional spaces. Table 5.5 gives mean integration values by room function for both components. In figure 5.20, the living and storage room values from table 5.5 are pre-

TABLE 5.5

Mean Integration Values by Function for Components I and II

Roomblock and Component	Living	Storage	Living Converted to Storage	Living or Storage	Ceremonial	Ceremonial Storage
16, I	1.136 ($n = 8$)	1.099 ($n = 7$)	1.125 ($n = 1$)	—	0.962 ($n = 1$)	1.125 ($n = 1$)
18, I	1.037 ($n = 9$)	1.028 ($n = 7$)	1.119 ($n = 7$)	1.033 ($n = 1$)	0.978 ($n = 1$)	—
5–6, I	1.039 ($n = 5$)	0.991 ($n = 2$)	1.047 ($n = 5$)	1.154 ($n = 2$)	1.089 ($n = 1$)	1.224 ($n = 1$)
16, II	1.503 ($n = 10$)	1.618 ($n = 5$)	—	1.224 ($n = 1$)	0.961 ($n = 1$)	—
9, II	1.255 ($n = 4$)	1.711 ($n = 2$)	—	1.800 ($n = 1$)	0.955 ($n = 1$)	—
10, II	1.277 ($n = 3$)	—	—	1.328 ($n = 1$)	1.176 ($n = 1$)	—

sented as box plots. The pattern of relatively small differences between storage and living rooms during Component I is reversed during Component II. Whereas the mean integration values for Component I storage and living rooms are comparable, the mean values for Component II storage rooms are consistently higher (in the two roomblocks for which data are available) than those for living rooms. In other words, the overall trend toward higher integration values in the roomblocks correlates with a trend toward greater variance between storage and living rooms. This finding underscores the inference that fundamental notions about the arrangement of space within the pueblo had undergone a significant change.

In an unpublished architectural analysis of Arroyo Hondo Pueblo, John D. Beal (1971:88) wrote that judging from "data obtained in 1971, Coalition Period [Component I] rooms are extensively interrelated, whereas Classic Period [Component II] rooms usually form two-room units." Space syntax analysis not only supports Beal's assertion but also quantifies it. The analysis shows three concomitant trends between Components I and II: an overall shift toward greater spatial

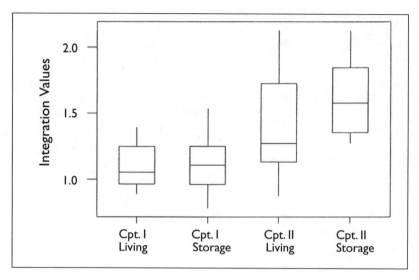

Figure 5.20. Box plots comparing mean integration values for living and storage rooms, Components I and II.

segregation within roomblocks, increased focus on plazas as primary integrating spaces, and greater differentiation between the integration values of living rooms and storage rooms. In the following chapter I explore the meaning of these trends in the context of Arroyo Hondo's history.

6
Interpretations and Comparisons

Spatial analysis has, as one of its aims, the measurement of a building or settlement
in units or patterns that allow interpretation and comparison with other sites. In
other words, spatial analysis generates ways of seeing and understanding.
—*Graham Fairclough, "Meaningful Constructions: Spatial and*
Functional Analysis of Medieval Buildings"

Correlating observed changes in architecture with concurrent changes in social and political organization is not a new direction in Southwestern archaeology. This study is merely another step along a path blazed by T. Mitchell Prudden (1903), Arthur Rohn (1965), David Wilcox (1975), and R. Gwinn Vivian (1990). The application of space syntax analysis to Arroyo Hondo Pueblo has shown that between Components I and II, a discernible shift took place toward greater spatial segregation—that is, more privacy—within roomblocks; people began to place greater emphasis on plazas as public community spaces; and the relationship between living rooms and storage rooms underwent a shift.

There are at least two possible explanations for the observed differences. Either a new group of people arrived to build and occupy the Component II settlement with a different view of how roomblock space should be arranged, or else descendants of the original

Component I inhabitants returned with new ideas on the same subject. Tantalizing indications that Arroyo Hondo Pueblo was never completely abandoned (Wetterstrom 1986), together with strong similarities in material culture between the components, suggest that the latter explanation is the more plausible (Habicht-Mauche 1993). If one assumes that some of the original inhabitants or their descendants returned to Arroyo Hondo in the 1370s, then something had changed within the span of a couple of generations to orient those people toward a more segregated conception of domestic space.

Depth indicates control. Contemporary vernacular housing places bedrooms and bathrooms in the deepest spaces, illustrating the value of personal privacy for certain activities (Brown and Steadman 1991). Business organizations place the chief executive in the deepest spot, often literally above, in terms of floors, and beyond spaces reserved for clerks, secretaries, and lesser executives. In the late prehistoric Southwest, the deepest structures have been consistently identified as storage facilities (Bustard 1995; Shapiro 1997, 1999; Fangmeier 1998), and Arroyo Hondo is no exception. If it is reasonable to assume that activities conducted in the deepest spaces are among the most private or restricted, then one could infer that individual storage of food gained increased importance at Arroyo Hondo during Component II, as opposed to more accessible, public, communal storage during Component I. A spatial structure that reflects increased control over and decreased access to selected resources implies that unrestricted sharing was not part of the economic system during Component II, despite economic uncertainty and a general need for cooperation.

Notwithstanding the close day-to-day association among tightly packed households—even in the relatively small Component II settlement—private space was maintained in the front-to-back connections that limited access into portions of residence units. Plazas and kivas were where group activities took place, much as they do today. It is conceivable that while public plazas served to integrate groups at the larger, community scale, an opposite movement took place toward social segregation at the scale of individual domestic units. Even though the Component II residences are close together, walls and openings were arranged so as to restrict accessibility and the probability of social encounters.

Measuring connectedness reveals how, over time, plazas integrated and unified numerous, similarly structured roomblocks. In the more segregated Component II roomblocks, front-to-back linkages were strengthened so that the movement of people, energy, and information flowed to and from the plazas. The plazas occupied relatively shallow locations within the spatial networks but exercised control over access to the interior spaces. In contrast, none of the Component I spaces had the same combination of integration and control values as the Component II plazas. Component I roomblocks were characterized by more circuitous linkages that facilitated internal circulation and communication. Over the span of the Coalition and Classic periods, then, spatial patterns became more asymmetrical and branched, reflecting the dichotomy between controlling spaces (integrated public plazas) and potentially controllable spaces (segregated private rooms and suites). All activities in the plaza could be seen, heard, or smelled and, in a broad sense, controlled. Private activities within individual family apartments were not subject to such communitywide observation and control. Thus, tensions between individual family groups and the larger community were both expressed and ameliorated by architecture.

The archaeological record supports a conclusion that at Arroyo Hondo everyone, during both components, shared essentially the same lifestyle, yet space syntax analysis indicates progressive spatial segregation among residential roomblocks and an increasing significance of plazas as spaces of communitywide cohesion. Perhaps the material manifestations were not so different, but by the 1370s and 1380s residents seem to have enjoyed less potential freedom of movement. If built space within roomblocks was becoming increasingly private, then some kind of mechanism must have existed to facilitate community decision-making. Gregory Johnson's (1989) sequential hierarchy model, which stresses shared authority among social segments, is consistent with archaeological, ethnographic, and spatial interpretations of Arroyo Hondo. Some limited and situational authority might have been exercised by a few "segment leaders," but no single segment appears to have dominated the sociopolitical structure.

Irrespective of whether the material remains indicate a relatively egalitarian social structure (Palkovich 1980; Habicht-Mauche 1993), some type of emergent hierarchy might still have been operating at Arroyo Hondo. Component II's more segregated spatial organization might be the physical manifestation of a hierarchy expressed through esoteric religious knowledge (see, e.g., Upham 1982, 1988; Smith 1983) rather than through "chiefly" residences or specialized mortuary

93

treatments (Howell 1996). Morton Fried's definition of an egalitarian society as "one where there are as many positions of prestige in any given age-sex grade as there are persons capable of filling them" (Fried 1967:33) has been quoted with almost scriptural consistency, but an equally acceptable definition is that of a society in which "members have essentially equal access to critical resources and a relatively unre- stricted flow of information about those resources" (Gumerman and Dean 1989:132). If access to selected built spaces is viewed as a limit- ed resource, then the evolution of spatial control and restriction at Arroyo Hondo offers the possibility that traditional indicators of sociopolitical complexity may not reveal all the ways in which social differentiation was marked.

COMPARISONS WITH OTHER NORTHERN RIO GRANDE SETTLEMENTS

Tijeras Pueblo (LA 581)

The findings from Arroyo Hondo, while intriguing, may be even more useful as the basis for new hypotheses regarding the relationship between architectural and cultural evolution throughout the northern Rio Grande region. To formalize such hypotheses, it is necessary to compare the data from Arroyo Hondo with data from other ancestral Pueblo communities in the region. Tijeras Pueblo is a large, well-exca- vated pueblo with occupation dates paralleling those of Arroyo Hondo and an archaeological record amenable to space syntax analysis.

Tijeras Pueblo (figs. 6.1 and 6.2) was located in Tijeras Canyon, a natural pass through the Sandia and Manzano Mountains, approxi- mately 10 miles east of present-day Albuquerque, New Mexico. Some- time between 1300 and 1400 C.E., the canyon's population increased and consolidated at the site of Tijeras Pueblo (Cordell 1975:10–12). Tijeras was occupied for approximately the same period as Arroyo Hondo (roughly 1300–1425) but was a much smaller settlement, con- sisting of slightly more than 130 rooms at its greatest extent (Judge 1973:43). Like Arroyo Hondo, Tijeras underwent a period of initial growth at the beginning of the fourteenth century, followed by decline and partial abandonment and, finally, rebuilding during the late 1300s (Cordell 1975:27, Cordell, ed., 1980:11, 181). Unlike Arroyo Hondo, Tijeras Pueblo never went through a period of complete abandonment and reoccupation.

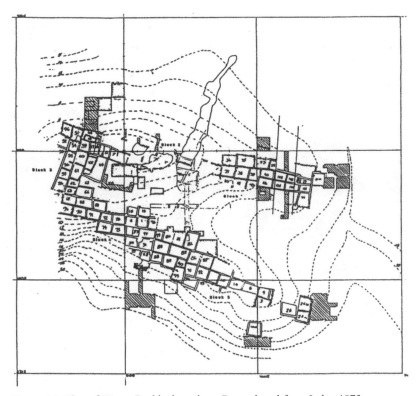

Figure 6.1. Plan of Tijeras Pueblo, late phase. Reproduced from Judge 1973.

Tijeras was excavated during the early 1970s, and several publications detailed aspects of its ecological setting and cultural evolution (Judge 1973; Cordell 1977a, 1977b, Cordell, ed., 1980). The research questions asked at Tijeras were somewhat different from those pursued at Arroyo Hondo, and therefore the available data set emphasizes slightly dissimilar issues. Nevertheless, sufficient data were available for a syntactic analysis that provides a meaningful comparison between the two sites.

Figure 6.3 is a plan of roomblocks 3, 4, 5, and a portion of 2 as they would have appeared during the late occupation at Tijeras Pueblo (ca. 1400–1425).[1] Only about 30 percent of the site was excavated, so architectural details such as doorways and upper-story spaces in unexcavated areas are subject to the same kinds of informed speculation that were applied to Arroyo Hondo. A summary of roomblock data for Tijeras Pueblo is given in Appendix B.

95

Figure 6.2. Tijeras Canyon, looking west from the upper end of the gorge through the pass between Sandia and Manzano mountains (neg. no. 2A23682, photograph by N. C. Nelson, courtesy Department of Library Services, the American Museum of Natural History).

Rather than a series of orthogonal roomblocks arranged around multiple plazas, roomblocks occupied during this late phase at Tijeras were arranged around a single, elongated plaza. Aside from the construction and abandonment of a number of outlying units, the essential shape of the pueblo remained largely unchanged, consisting of a U-shaped concretion of single-story units, together with some two- and three-story rooms, around the plaza. Although Tijeras exhibits similarities of form with both components at Arroyo Hondo, it is distinguishable in a number of ways, such as in having rectangular kivas or ceremonial rooms placed within the roomblock rather than having circular kivas in plazas.[2] As in the case of Arroyo Hondo's Component I, excavations at Tijeras revealed a pattern of lateral doorways that permits an inference of lateral movement through the roomblocks. Unlike Arroyo Hondo, where virtually all first-story structures were entered from rooftop hatchways, Tijeras had at least four ground-floor doorways that opened directly onto the plaza.

At Arroyo Hondo, the architectural and temporal separation between Components I and II was reasonably clear, but for Tijeras it

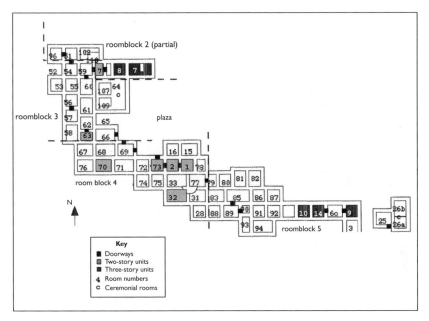

Figure 6.3. Schematic plan of Tijeras Pueblo, late phase, roomblocks 3, 4, and 5 and a portion of roomblock 2.

was more difficult to separate the occupation history into periods or components. Nonetheless, Linda Cordell (1996:236) described the importance of understanding diachronic changes as Tijeras Pueblo developed from a series of irregularly spaced, small roomblocks into a large, connected structure. She noted that "if previous site organization is not examined, the final buildings at big sites may manifest a degree of organization that can misleadingly suggest in-migration rather than the spatial reorganization of existing populations" (Cordell 1996:236). This observation is well taken, but at least for the initial stages of space syntax analysis, the focus is less on where a pueblo's inhabitants came from than on the ways in which they arranged their built space.

Figure 6.4 is a justified access diagram of the portion of Tijeras Pueblo depicted in figure 6.3. Because of the large number of rooms, together with the presence of second- and third-story spaces, the diagram is complicated, but I believe it reasonably represents the room relationships. Consistent with the analysis of Arroyo Hondo, all doorways were considered to have been open contemporaneously, and to

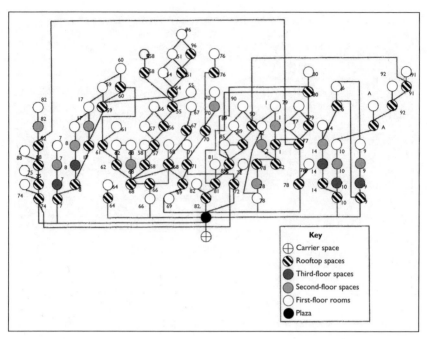

Figure 6.4. Justified access graph for the Tijeras Pueblo roomblocks shown in figure 6.3.

the extent that there was any bias in terms of potential pathways, nodal connections (i.e., potential encounters) were favored.

Table 6.1 summarizes the numerical values obtained from the space syntax analysis of figure 6.4. (A complete list of integration and control values appears in Appendix C.) When compared with the data from Arroyo Hondo, the data from Tijeras (or, more accurately, Tijeras, late phase) exhibit significant differences with Arroyo Hondo Component I and significant affinities with Component II.[3] Figures 6.5 and 6.6 portray this information in box plots that compare mean integration values for individual roomblocks at the two sites and for Tijeras and Arroyo Hondo Components I and II as wholes. Despite the existence of connections among what appear to be suites of rooms, Tijeras's overall integration value of 1.25 is high enough to suggest a substantial degree of spatial segregation. As in some roomblocks at Arroyo Hondo, alternative pathways among spaces at Tijeras are sufficiently deep within the structure to make some spaces relatively inaccessible from the carrier space.

98

TABLE *6.1*

Summary of Integration Values for Tijeras Pueblo

No. Spaces	No. Links	Mean Integration Value	Node with Lowest Value	Node with Highest Value	High-Low Difference
115	135	1.25	0.64	1.94	1.30

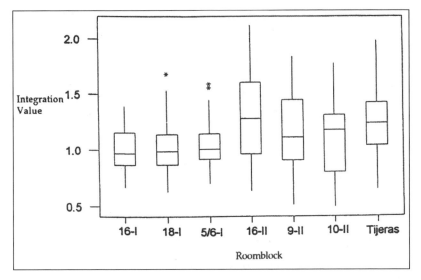

Figure 6.5. Box plots comparing mean integration values for individual roomblocks at Arroyo Hondo Pueblo and Tijeras Pueblo.

Figures 6.5 and 6.6, in conjunction with table 6.1, reveal a consistency between the mean integration value of Tijeras's late phase roomblocks and the mean integration values for Arroyo Hondo's Component II roomblocks. This finding is supported by a review of the distribution of integration values. Table 6.2 shows that the pattern observed for Tijeras replicates that for Component II at Arroyo Hondo, particularly in terms of the numbers of rooms that had relatively high integration values.

As at Component II Arroyo Hondo, the plaza at Tijeras had the lowest integration value (see Appendix C) and therefore can be considered

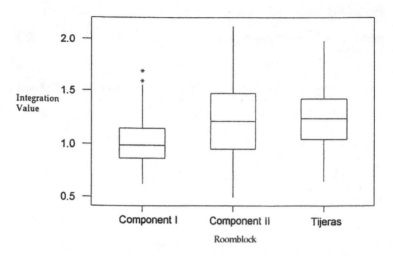

Figure 6.6. Box plots comparing mean integration values for Components I and II, Arroyo Hondo Pueblo, and Tijeras Pueblo.

the shallowest and most integrating space in the settlement. This finding is not surprising, given the single-plaza format at Tijeras, but even though Tijeras was basically an accretional settlement, with individual rooms or groups of rooms added over time, its resulting form reflected a deliberate decision on the part of those responsible for the pueblo's construction to develop the plaza as the primary focal space.

Tijeras also exhibits the same pattern of integration values by room function as Arroyo Hondo Component II. Table 6.3 provides the mean value by room function for a series of Tijeras rooms. The categories are not precisely the same as those used at Arroyo Hondo, but the most significant classifications—habitation, storage, and ceremonial—are reasonably consonant. As in the case of Arroyo Hondo Component II, storage spaces have a higher mean integration value than do habitation spaces, but unlike at Arroyo Hondo, ceremonial spaces have an intermediate value. It is interesting that the Tijeras kiva (room 64) revealed a more moderate integration value (0.50) than did a ceremonial room embedded in the roomblock (room 6, with a value of 1.00), presumably because access to the specialized ceremonial room was more limited.

A consistent use pattern at Tijeras Pueblo placed storage rooms in relatively less accessible and more controllable spaces than habitation rooms. Moreover, the overall degree of differentiation between Tijeras'

TABLE 6.2

Distribution of Integration Values for Tijeras and Arroyo Hondo
Pueblos

	Number of Spaces		
Integration Value	Arroyo Hondo, CI (*n* = 174)	Arroyo Hondo, CII (*n* = 81)	Tijeras (*n* = 115)
0–0.500	—	1	—
0.501–1.000	91	24	21
1.001–1.500	79	37	72
1.501–2.000	4	17	22
2.001–2.500	—	2	—

TABLE 6.3

Mean Integration Values by Room Function for Tijeras Pueblo

Room Function	Mean Integration Value
Storage (*n* = 15)	1.39
Habitation (*n* = 19)	1.21
Habitation or storage (*n* = 4)	1.23
Habitation/ceremonial (*n* = 3)	1.18
Ceremonial (*n* = 2)	1.26
Special use—food processing (*n* = 3)	1.53

Note: The Tijeras data were taken directly from Room Excavation Summary Forms (Blevins and Atwood 1974), which did not note functions for every room. In the case of multistory units, some excavation forms assigned specific functions to individual floors. In other cases, all floors were given the same classification. The classification "habitation/ceremonial" includes one three-story space (room 14) for which the room summary report does not indicate separate floor functions.

habitation and storage rooms fell between the values of the two Arroyo Hondo components. Because Tijeras was built more incrementally than Arroyo Hondo, it is not surprising that some of its integration values are intermediate to those of the Arroyo Hondo sets. Nonetheless, the overall values and patterns seen at Tijeras show greater affinity with those from Arroyo Hondo Component II than with those of Component I.

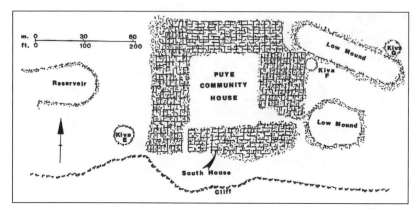

Figure 6.7. Map of Puyé, 1907 (after a drawing by William Boone Douglas; Peckham 1996).

A correlation is not an explanation, but the data from the late phase at Tijeras support the findings from Arroyo Hondo concerning spatial segregation and the increasing importance of plazas. Something was happening in the northern Rio Grande region during the late fourteenth and early fifteenth centuries that resulted in spatial arrangements that stressed the integrating value of plazas and the segregating value of residential roomblocks. Whether it was the katsina cult, the stresses born of substantial population increase and dislocation, or some other factor, the effect was to change the manner in which pueblos were arranged.

Puyé Pueblo

Another example of ancestral Pueblo architecture is the South House at Puyé Pueblo, near the present-day pueblo of Santa Clara, New Mexico (fig. 6.7). Puyé sits on an isolated mesa and includes a large, rectangular, Classic-period community house, several smaller Coalition-period structures, and a number of "caveate" dwellings along the margins of the mesa, particularly on the southern side (Morley 1910; Hewett 1938; Peckham 1996). The only portion of the site to which space syntax analysis was applied was the South House, a free-standing portion of the Classic-period community house (fig. 6.8).[4]

The South House was excavated in 1907 and 1909 under the auspices of Edgar L. Hewett and the School of American Archaeology

102

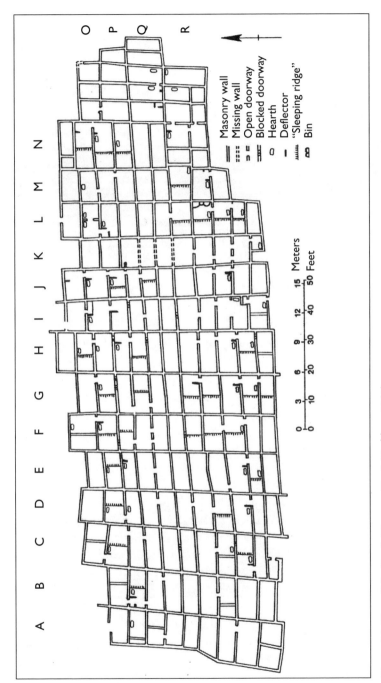

Figure 6.8. Plan of the South House at Puyé (Peckham 1996).

Figure 6.9. Puyé ruins in 1910 (Jesse L. Nussbaum, courtesy Palace of the Governors [MNM/DCA] neg. no. 358).

(now the School of American Research) in Santa Fe. Virtually the entire structure was excavated and found to consist of 173 ground-floor rooms arranged in 14 parallel, north–south rows of approximately 10 to 12 rooms each (figs. 6.8 and 6.9). There appeared to have been an east–west wall through the structure that separated the rooms into two groups, approximately half of them oriented toward the north and half toward the south. Although the excavators noted the likely presence of upper stories, archaeological confirmation of the numbers, sizes, and locations of such rooms is much more equivocal than it is for either Arroyo Hondo or Tijeras Pueblo. Sylvanus Morley (1910:8) was clear in his belief that as many as 50 second-story and some third-story rooms existed, but hard evidence is simply unavailable to permit the kind of analysis that was possible for Arroyo Hondo and Tijeras. Therefore, no upper stories were configured into the space syntax analysis.

Internal doorways were numerous in the South House and, with a few exceptions, followed a strict front-to-back pattern. These arrangements created a series of separate units whose access was through the single enclosed plaza. The relative paucity of doorways opening directly onto the plaza suggests that most of the units were entered via ladders and hatchways.

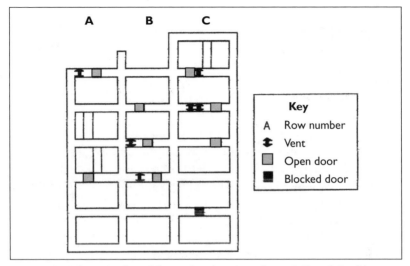

Figure 6.10. Schematic plan of the northern portion of rows A, B, and C of the South House, Puyé Pueblo.

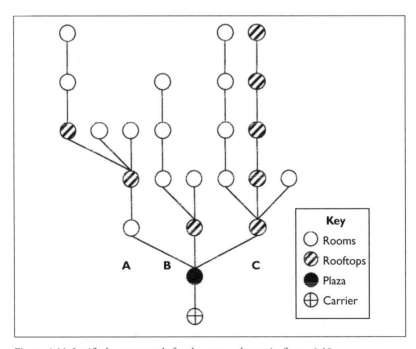

Figure 6.11. Justified access graph for the spaces shown in figure 6.10.

The South House was a planned construction project. With the exception of its most recent, eastern section, most of the building was built as a unit, albeit in a series of stages. In consideration of the size of the South House, I analyzed three sample sections. The results revealed a series of branched and highly segregated domestic spatial arrangements whose overall permeability was much more limited than even that of Arroyo Hondo's Component II.

Figure 6.10 depicts the northern portion of rows A, B, and C of the South House, and figure 6.11 is the justified access graph for those sections. The graph has an asymmetrical, nondistributed, and highly branched appearance and a relatively high mean integration value of 1.59. All the doorways and vents emphasized front-to-back connections, and there were no circuits within this portion of the South House.

Figure 6.12 is a plan of the northern portion of rows H, I, and J of the South House. Its justified access graph (fig. 6.13) is even more asymmetrical, nondistributed, and branched than the graph for the preceding section. The long series of front-to-back doorways isolates the deepest rooms, and in the absence of any lateral openings, the very high mean integration value of 1.80 is not unexpected.

Despite some obvious similarities, there are subtle differences in spatial arrangements between the earlier parts of the South House and the later, eastern section (figs. 6.14, 6.15). In contrast to the rest of South House, the eastern section exhibited a more distributed spatial arrangement that may largely result from the presence of lateral doorways, features that were otherwise absent at South House. The mean integration value of 1.36, while still relatively high, is lower than those of the other two sections. The overall plan still stressed spatial segregation, yet the specific arrangements imply that those responsible for building the eastern section had different ideas about organizing space from those of the original builders. Although hardly a circuitous structure, this section is definitely more highly circuited than the others. Its mean integration value is closer to those of Arroyo Hondo Component II and Tijeras Pueblo than to those of the other sections at Puyé. A coincidence, perhaps, but archaeological evidence has indicated that the eastern section was built as part of an early-sixteenth-century reoccupation by Southern Tewa (Tano) people (Peckham 1996:156, 167). As such, the builders of this eastern section might have shared social, economic, or ethnic affiliations with the builders of Arroyo Hondo and Tijeras.

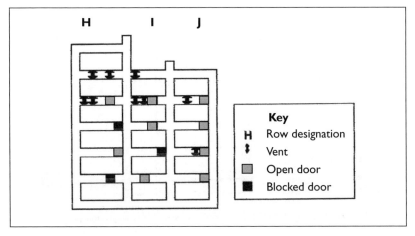

Figure 6.12. Schematic plan of the northern portion of rows H, I, and J of the South House, Puyé Pueblo.

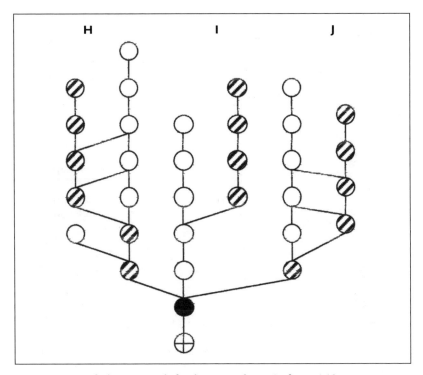

Figure 6.13. Justified access graph for the spaces shown in figure 6.12.

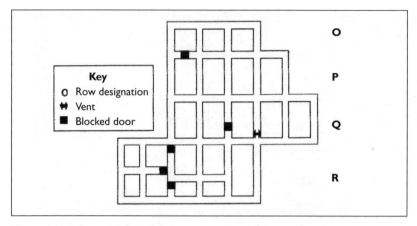

Figure 6.14. Schematic plan of the eastern portion of the South House, Puyé Pueblo.

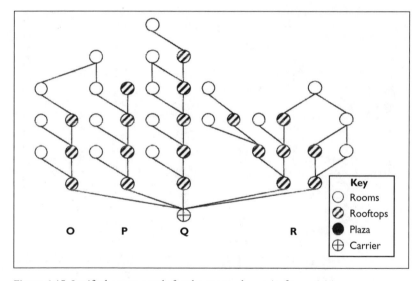

Figure 6.15. Justified access graph for the spaces shown in figure 6.14.

A COMPARISON WITH ACOMA PUEBLO

The absence of clear information about upper-story spaces restricted the analysis of Puyé to first-floor rooms. Although analyses limited to the ground floors in multistory structures have been successfully conducted at Chaco Canyon (Cooper 1995), a better model for the segregated, front-to-back room arrangements that typified Classic-period pueblos in the northern Rio Grande may lie just outside that region, in the form of Acoma Pueblo. Situated on an isolated mesa about 60 miles west of Albuquerque, New Mexico (figs. 6.16 and 6.17), this western Keresan pueblo vies with Taos and the Hopi village of Old Oraibi for the title of the oldest continually occupied settlement in North America. The site was probably settled some time in the thirteenth century; Acoma oral accounts, supported by archaeological data, refer to four separate ancestral groups that coalesced to form the pueblo at some earlier, undefined time.

One of the best, and still sound, physical descriptions of Acoma was provided by Leslie White (1929:29), who observed:

> The houses are built on the bare surface of the rock. They are arranged in three long rows, with a few scattered between. All houses in the rows face south. The top floor is used as a living room; cooking is done here on a fireplace. The middle floor is used partly as a sleeping-living room and partly as a storeroom. Until recently, there were no openings in the walls of the rooms on the ground floor; one ascended ladders to the upper floors and then went down ladders through trapdoors to the floors below.

White's description only hints at the highly segregated spatial arrangement that space syntax analysis suggests is a reflection of Acoma's social segregation. More explicit is a statement by White's contemporary, Mrs. W. T. Sedgwick (1926:20): "Though in appearance the long blocks of apartments are community houses, they are in no sense communal if that term be used to define a socialistic form of life. Each family or clan is a unit completely separated from every other by very solid division walls. Independence of all but the immediate family or clan can hardly be carried to a greater extreme than with the Indian."

In 1934 Acoma was visited by members of the Historic American Buildings Survey (HABS), who made a series of detailed drawings of the entire settlement. The drawings were concentrated on the facades of the buildings but also included a few examples of the internal room arrangements in private residences. The two most extensively documented residences were North Building, Block 1, Unit 3 (fig. 6.18) and Middle Building, Block 6, Unit 4 (fig. 6.19), both of which were

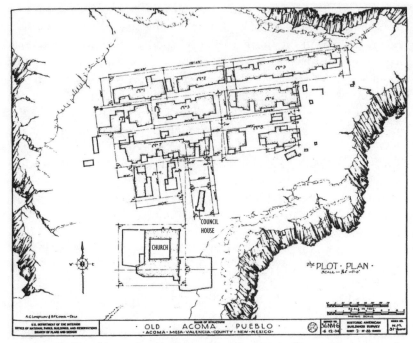

Figure 6.16. Plan of Acoma Pueblo. Reproduced from United States Department of the Interior 1934, sheet 79.

Figure 6.17. Acoma Pueblo, ca. 1882 (Ben Wittick, courtesy Palace of the Governors [MNM/DCA] neg. no. 16044).

TABLE *6.4*

Mean Integration Values for Acoma Pueblo

House No.	No. Spaces	No. Links	Mean Integration Value	Low Integration Value	High Integration Value	High-Low Difference
Block 6, Unit 4	11	11	1.41	0.68	2.11	1.43
Block 3, Unit 2	16	16	1.76	1.06	3.11	2.05
Block 1, Unit 3	16	15	1.93	1.06	3.11	2.05

described as "typical dwellings" in the original HABS report (United States Department of the Interior 1934). These units were recorded in such detail that virtually all built spaces, room functions, and interroom openings were noted. The average integration values for the two structures are relatively high (table 6.4), indicating considerable spatial segregation. The spatial arrangements for both structures involve tree- or candelabra-shaped graphs, with very little "ringiness." Although most of the individual integration values are well in excess of 1.00, the lowest values are associated with plazas, terraces, and rooftops. The most highly segregated spaces are invariably storage spaces. Living, sleeping, and kitchen spaces generally exhibit intermediate values.

Figure 6.19, the justified access graph for Block 1, Unit 3, illustrates these points. The mean integration value (1.93) indicates a very segregated spatial arrangement. This finding is buttressed by the absence of any alternative access pathways within this unit, which, despite the number of built spaces (15) and connections (15), is an exceedingly private arrangement.

The justified access graph for Block 6, Unit 4 (figs. 6.20 and 6.21), takes a form not quite so candelabra-like as the preceding example, but its mean integration value (1.41) is still indicative of very segregated and private space. There is a single shallow ring, but, in general, there are no alternative pathways through this structure.

Finally, Block 3, Unit 2, was also well documented, though less extensively than the other two units. Nevertheless, its basic organizational pattern is consistent with the preceding structures in terms of

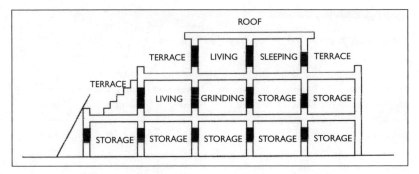

Figure 6.18. Schematic plan of Block 1, Unit 3, at Acoma Pueblo. Adapted from from United States Department of the Interior 1934.

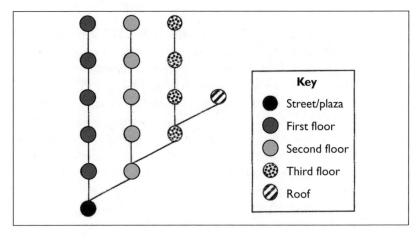

Figure 6.19. Justified access graph for the spaces shown in figure 6.18.

room functions and a high degree of spatial segregation (fig. 6.22). The mean integration value, 1.76, is midway between those of the other two structures.

Insofar as rooftops are concerned, there appear to have been no generalized pathways across connected rooftops at Acoma Pueblo in 1934. This view is supported by photographs that do not show rooftops being used as paths, as they were at Zuni. To travel from one house to another, it was necessary to go back down to the street or plaza level. Each residence was independent of its neighbors, but they were all tied together through the integrating functions of the plazas.

The integration values for the three Acoma units show affinities

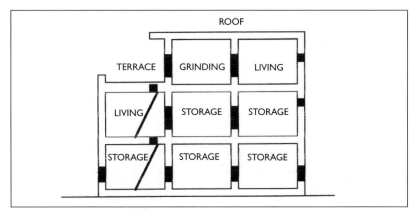

Figure 6.20. Schematic plan of Block 6, Unit 4, at Acoma Pueblo. Adapted from from United States Department of the Interior 1934.

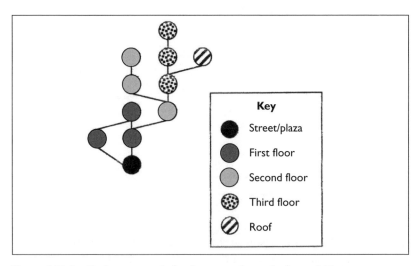

Figure 6.21. Justified access graph for the spaces shown in figure 6.20.

with those for Arroyo Hondo, Tijeras, and especially Puyé. The Acoma data support the argument that the form of spatial organization that first became manifest during the late fourteenth century set a pattern that persisted into historic times.[5] The integration values argue not only for the continuation of these architectural forms but also for a strengthening of them, for these numbers indicate greater spatial segregation than that at any of the other analyzed pueblos.

113

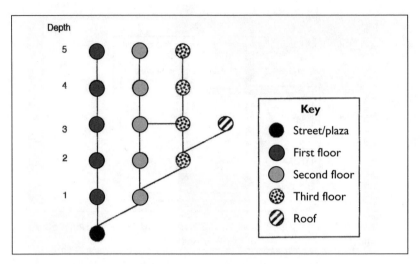

Figure 6.22. Justified access graph for Block 3, Unit 2, at Acoma Pueblo.

TABLE *6.5*

Mean Integration Values by Room Function for Acoma Pueblo

Room Function	Mean Integration Value
Living ($n = 7$)	1.39
Roof/terrace ($n = 9$)	1.47
Grinding ($n = 2$)	1.59
Sleeping ($n = 2$)	1.94
Storage ($n = 19$)	2.02

A functional comparison of the Acoma rooms exemplifies the kind of "layering" characteristic of traditional Pueblo architecture, in which selected domestic activities were assigned to certain locations (table 6.5). Storage rooms have the highest mean integration values. Considering White's comment about the absence of doorways between ground-floor rooms, it is likely that some storage spaces were even more highly segregated in the past, so the overall integration values would have been even higher. The lowest mean values are associated with living rooms. Granted, the mean value for those rooms is much higher than at any of the prehistoric sites, but the fundamental pattern observed at Arroyo Hondo appears to hold.

THE RELATIONSHIP OF SPATIAL AND SOCIAL STRUCTURES IN THE NORTHERN RIO GRANDE

Numerous investigators have commented on the patterned changes involving architecture, social organization, and ideographic symbolism that took place in the northern Rio Grande region during the thirteenth, fourteenth, and fifteenth centuries (e.g., Cordell 1989b, 1996; Crown, Orcutt, and Kohler 1996). These changes were both widespread and persistent, suggesting the existence of either fundamental rules or a constellation of shared experiences that guided behavior. One potential and largely overlooked explanation for the adoption of plaza-and-roomblock-style settlements is a kind of social stress caused by a juxtaposition of different ethnic groups almost literally thrown together by social and economic dislocations. The observation that change leads to anxiety may sound like a truism, but it seems to resonate with some validity. For small, closed societies to operate successfully, they need a certain level of what might be called "common civility." In Pueblo societies, such concepts are embodied in unwritten codes that stress group harmony above individual expression (Ortiz 1969). When ancestral Pueblo people of diverse ethnic backgrounds found themselves living in larger, aggregated settlements, they probably experienced increased social tension. Various ideological mechanisms have been considered as ways in which these new communities might have been integrated (Adams 1991; Crown 1994; Herr and Clark 1997), but only limited consideration has been given to the physical arrangement of architecture as an integrative mechanism (Ferguson 1996).

Architectural developments that resulted in a continuum of public and private space offered a way to deal with such stresses when neither the physical nor the social environment provided an outlet. A combination of controlled-access, open plazas and spatially segregated roomblocks enabled resident kin-based groups to spatially delineate a familiar environment yet still be part of the larger settlement. The process is analogous to what the Aztecs did at Tenochtitlan with their *calpulli* and the Inkas did at Cuzco with their *ayllus*, two forms of kin-based corporate social units. Those situations involved state-imposed, designated neighborhoods, but they were geographically based systems that replicated and strengthened long-standing corporate and kinship ties.[6]

While one must be wary of applying contemporary behavioral

115

theories to prehistoric situations, one field of research from which ideas about crowding might provide useful analogs involves migration into areas that are already occupied (Greenbie 1974; Sherrod and Cohen 1978). It is generally accepted that large-scale population movements took place throughout the Southwest at various times from the thirteenth through the seventeenth centuries. These movements involved not only ancestral Pueblo people but also Mogollon groups from southwestern New Mexico, Numic (Ute) groups from the west, and Athabaskan (Navajo and Apache) groups from the north. Irrespective of whether the genesis of those movements was intraregional or interregional, the construction, abandonment, reoccupation, and reconstruction of settlements in the northern Rio Grande region during the Coalition and Classic periods is not disputed.

Migration, aggregation, warfare, trade, and the spread of the katsina cult all presuppose a substantial amount of social interaction. How such contact was regulated, how privacy was maintained, and how "foreign" intrusions were minimized might be partly explainable by considering architectural changes in response to crowding. It has been found that the stresses associated with crowding are culturally mediated (Hall 1966; Loo 1977), though I am not conflating contemporary urban congestion with fourteenth-century Pueblo lifeways. Nevertheless, it can hardly be coincidental that patterns reflecting increasing spatial segregation in ancestral Pueblo villages appear at the same time that environmental and social perturbations were increasing competition for limited resources (Haas and Creamer 1996; Walsh 1998) or that ideological changes, most notably expressed in the katsina cult, were operating to facilitate control within groups (Adams 1991; Hodder 1991:21). As noted in the preceding chapter, we are looking at longterm processes that began to appear during the occupation of Arroyo Hondo Component I and became much more apparent during Component II. In other words, the architectural changes that can be traced through the Coalition and Classic periods in the northern Rio Grande were long-term societal adaptations to a variety of increased environmental and social demands.

The decision to move or stay in a particular place is related to the presence of stress "generated by interpersonal relations or by uncontrolled fluctuations in the physical world" (Wolpert 1966:95). Environmental psychologists have posited that when interpersonal stress reaches a certain level, people may simply pick up and move.

According to contemporary studies of intra-urban migration, it is the inability to modify or counteract stress that ultimately leads to a change in residence (Michelson 1970:27). The same concept that psychologists use to define the idea of privacy—namely, the ability to control the level and intensity of social interactions (Hall 1966; Altman and Chemers 1980; Rapoport 1980)—has been offered to explain the social dislocations caused by migrations. Edward T. Hall's proxemic theory holds that one's perceived control over physical stimuli within a bounded space is important for psychological well-being (Hall 1966). When one loses the ability to avoid unwanted interactions, one feels a "loss of privacy" that may contribute to stress-related problems at an individual or a societal scale (Hall 1966). Hall's proxemics are culturally based, but every society ultimately resorts to some mechanisms in order to cope with a real or perceived loss of control and allow the social organization to be maintained (Wolpert 1966:94–95; Markus 1972).

The idea of populations in flux relocating within a landscape of limited resources may explain why some prehistoric Southwestern groups began to feel crowded. Information overload (having too much new communication or stimulation suddenly imposed), constraints on freedom to behave in a customary manner, and a scarcity of resources as more people arrive and make demands are three empirically observed results of migration (Bell, Fisher, and Loomia 1978).

Large-scale coping mechanisms may include architectural intervention to provide escape from excessive stimulation, changes in organizational structures to create new ways to manage the social landscape, and increased expressions of territorial exclusivity (Stokols 1976; Bell, Fisher, and Loomia 1978). All three classes of responses have a common purpose, that of avoiding "unwanted interaction by controlling who interacts with whom, when, where, and in what context" (Rapoport 1980:297). It is noteworthy that observed responses to crowding seem to replicate the events or behaviors that archaeologists have inferred. Simply stated, the behavioral patterns exhibited by groups living in the northern Rio Grande region following the population increases of the thirteenth and fourteenth centuries included warfare (Haas 1990; Wilcox and Haas 1994), the fissioning of settlements (Snead 1996), and the initiation of organizational and architectural changes.

I am not the first to suggest a relationship between architectural design elements and the idea of privacy in the context of Southwest

117

prehistory. David Saile (1977:164–165) raised the possibility of Chacoan "town" (i.e., great-house) residents distinguishing themselves from outsiders through the use of low walls and open spaces that created privacy gradients. Karen Dohm (1990:232) posited an even more direct relationship between aggregation, house size, and the need for privacy: "Puebloans' need for privacy can be expected to vary more with population density differences than with cultural differences. Insofar as architectural nucleation is equivalent to within-village population nucleation, individuals' and families' use of more space and more rooms when housing is more aggregated indicates increased need for architectural solutions to the need for privacy with increased population aggregation."

Without necessarily agreeing with Dohm's view of population density versus cultural differences as determinants, I submit that a need for increasingly private spaces was a major motivating force for, as well as a deliberate by-product of, the architectural designs seen at Arroyo Hondo. It has been noted that "residential interiors with greater depth...will afford greater opportunities to regulate social interaction because inhabitants can more easily alter the degree of physical separation among themselves" (Evans, Lepore, and Schroeder 1996:42). The moderate spatial segregation seen during the Coalition period became much more pronounced during the Classic period. Throughout the northern Southwest, stressful conditions not only continued but also were exacerbated during Spanish colonization, with the result that settlements such as Acoma developed extremely segregated domestic spaces, a fundamental design that has persisted into historic times. The kinds of spatial organization seen at Arroyo Hondo may represent a Puebloan architectural response to a stressful and increasingly crowded social environment.

Analogous support for this view is found in a reexamination of the events collectively known as the "pithouse-to-pueblo transition," in which Southwestern people abandoned the use of semisubterranean structures in favor of aboveground masonry or adobe structures. Michelle Hegmon (1996:237, 240) showed that the architectural changes manifested during this transition were associated with increased privatization of food storage, which was, in turn, tied to external stresses of warfare and variable productivity caused by environmental perturbations. The kinds of stressors Hegmon described were most likely present in the northern Rio Grande during the Coalition and Classic periods as well, but they were not the only stressors. By the beginning of the fourteenth century, settlements were becoming larger, more densely populated, and fewer in number as occupation focused on areas with dependable water supplies (Dickson 1979; Crown, Orcutt, and Kohler 1996). These changes had organizational implications insofar as earlier modes of decision making might have been ineffective in the newly restructured communities (Bernardini 1996:2).

Coincident with these events, architectural modifications that enhanced a sense of control appeared throughout the northern Southwest as the physical design of large settlements changed from that of Chacoan-style great houses to more complex designs incorporating multiple roomblocks surrounding large public plazas (Jackson 1954; Swentzell 1988; Morgan 1994). Such designs afforded greater opportunity for different groups to live in communal settings without completely abrogating their ethnic or territorial integrity.

In addition to living areas within roomblocks, kivas underwent a change in both location and usage. Instead of being embedded within the massed rooms of great houses, new kivas were built in the plazas of ancestral Pueblo towns and villages.[7] Although the activities that took place inside the kivas remained segregated and private, kiva visitors could be identified and their comings and goings observed and monitored by the community at large. In addition, kivas' former multipurpose usages narrowed, and they became specialized ceremonial spaces associated with observances mediated by new religious organizations that cut across traditional lineage lines (Lekson 1988; Adams 1991). Despite their ongoing importance, in one sense kivas became auxiliary spaces to plazas, where the largest and most visible ceremonial events were conducted.

Space syntax analysis reveals that the integration values for kivas at Arroyo Hondo during both components were equal to or lower than the average integration values for individual roomblocks. If the kiva builders had intended kivas to be the most secure and protected spaces in the settlement, they would have located them in spatially deep areas. Instead, kivas were relatively exposed in the middle of plazas, where access was more a matter of social than of physical control. The physical location and relationship of kivas to the rest of the pueblo suggest a form of social control based on checks and balances such as might be manifested in a sequential hierarchy (Johnson 1983, 1989).

Architecture was one way of asserting spatial control at a time when new groups arrived in increasing numbers and often affiliated with preexisting settlements (see, generally, Loo 1977:162–165). This scenario does not assume a situation in which ranked or economically diverse classes were becoming meshed. Rather, this was a period of ethnic mixing akin to that described by Adolph Bandelier in his novel *The Delight Makers* (1971 [1890]), in which tribal or linguistically distinguishable but culturally similar groups found themselves living in the same settlements (e.g., Walsh 1998). These groups had to cooperate yet maintain their own definable enclaves against the social friction that resulted from proximity to other, co-resident groups. Archaeological evidence of social and architectural reorganization at later, proto-historic and historic pueblos illustrates the process of incorporation of smaller settlements into larger pueblos (Lycett 1994; Herr and Clark 1997). I suggest that the seventeenth- and eighteenth-century responses were repetitions of an earlier, fourteenth-century pattern that arose under similar conditions.

Earlier in this book I briefly discussed the recovery of social information from material remains and proposed some parallels between ceramic and architectural studies. In an examination of the nature of technology transfer, M. N. Zedeño (1994) surmised that differences between the quality of Pueblo III and Pueblo IV ceramics related to new residence patterns caused by population movements during the thirteenth and fourteenth centuries. "The striking variation in techno-logical knowledge, craftsmanship, and style evident in the decorated wares of Grasshopper Pueblo far surpasses that in ceramics from late Pueblo III period sites. This ceramic assemblage was largely a product of the heterogeneous social and ethnic makeup of large Pueblo IV period communities in east-central Arizona, and of their exchange or trade relations" (Zedeño 1994:131–132).

If new residence patterns and ethnic intermixing could stimulate the development of new ceramic technologies and styles, then the same processes could have stimulated analogous developments in archi-tectural forms and styles (Stark, Clark, and Elson 1995; Walsh 1998). Furthermore, if environmental stress can encourage innovation, as in the functional diversity of stone tool assemblages (Nelson 1996:109), then something as fundamental as architectural innovation may like-wise be seen as a response to increased stress in the social environment. Finally, if a variety of ideological and religious institutions functioned to integrate culturally heterogeneous groups (Herr and Clark 1997:368), then architecture could have operated similarly. As social and environmental pressures continued during the fourteenth and fifteenth centuries, the plaza-and-roomblock settlement form, with its increasingly public plazas and private living areas, might have been the best architectural adaptation to a new and more complicated social arena.

7
Conclusion

Whereness is concerned with linkages.
The legato of one squirrel holds a forest together.
—Frederick Sommer and Stephen Aldrich,
"The Poetic Logic of Art and Aesthetics"

Arroyo Hondo Pueblo was built and inhabited during a dynamic period in Southwestern prehistory. Whether one argues for intraregional or interregional migration into the northern Rio Grande region, persuasive archaeological evidence exists for large-scale population expansion and movement there during the thirteenth and fourteenth centuries. As new groups arrived in places that were already occupied, both the newcomers and the indigenous residents had to make adjustments to allow for peaceful interaction. At the same time, climatic perturbations limited the areas in which agriculturally reliant groups could establish permanent settlements.

These comments should not be taken to imply any downgrading of the potential for conflict and warfare that clearly characterized some of the relationships between immigrant and indigenous groups. Indeed, if warfare is viewed as one result of the stresses that develop from resource limitations as new groups "rub up against" one another, then warfare may be the flip side of the coin of social adaptation.

123

Architectural innovation is one way to accommodate changes in social organization and relieve some of the stresses that might lead to warfare. In the case of Arroyo Hondo and other, contemporaneous pueblos, the elaboration of new architectural forms may have enabled incoming groups to reclaim some of the autonomy they otherwise lost when they joined large, aggregated settlements.

Architectural changes are effective adaptations to the increased demands created by resource limitations that can characterize both the physical and social environments. Architecture can also provide a physical refuge that affords people an opportunity to retreat from these stressors (Hall 1966). In another, equally valid sense, architecture is a process that melds the utilitarian and the ideological (McGuire and Schiffer 1983). Ancestral Pueblo construction consisted of orthogonal roomblocks surrounding multiple plazas. Over time, changes occurred in the interior arrangements and layouts of similar-appearing roomblocks, in order to facilitate or inhibit social encounters. Although a pueblo might be viewed as a relatively stable, organic unit, the relationships among its constituent spaces vary over time. It follows that relationships among constituent social groups also vary over time. Architectural innovations enabled diverse groups to assert some measure of control over their immediate environment, thereby diffusing some of the stresses attendant upon rapid settlement aggregation.

Despite more than 100 years of architectural descriptions, only a handful of researchers in Southwestern archaeology have successfully drawn substantial information about social organization from the well-preserved architectural remains that dot the landscape. Many of the earlier studies focused on large, well-preserved masonry structures such as those found at Chaco Canyon, New Mexico (Vivian 1990), Mesa Verde, Colorado (Prudden 1903), and Wupatki, Arizona (Wilcox 1975). In the northern Rio Grande region, notwithstanding a long history of excavation (Nelson 1915a, 1915b; Jeançon 1923; Roberts 1935), equally few researchers have attempted to glean social information from pueblo sites. Beginning in the thirteenth century and continuing through Spanish colonization, Pueblo architecture underwent a series of changes that went hand-in-hand with a constellation of demographic and social changes. As a result of in-migration coupled with localized demographic expansion, populations increased dramatically and became increasingly aggregated in large settlements. The katsina cult was adopted throughout large portions of the region, presenting inhabitants with a new ideology that involved ceremonial activities carried out in both public plazas and more private spaces.

Arroyo Hondo Pueblo is well suited for a study comparing architectural and organizational changes, because its occupation bridged the gap between the Coalition (1200–1325 C.E.) and Classic (1325–1600) periods. Space syntax analysis reveals noticeable differences in the ways in which space was organized at Arroyo Hondo during its two components of habitation, including a significant shift toward greater residential "privacy" during Component II. These patterns are replicated in the space syntax analyses of the contemporaneously occupied pueblos of Tijeras and Puyé, as well as at Acoma Pueblo, the occupation of which continues to the present day.

Whereas many proffered explanations for cultural evolution in the Southwest continue to focus on the physical environment (e.g., Tainter and Tainter 1996), I suggest that the changes revealed in the archaeological record for the northern Rio Grande Valley reflect changes in the ability of resident groups to exercise control over parts of their social environment. If that is so, then space syntax analysis is one way to verify that the behavioral changes observed in the archaeological record are related to "society-directed" attempts to alleviate social stress and reassert "control" through changes in the built environment.

An analysis of the Component I architecture at Arroyo Hondo suggests that occupants of its "within-roomblock" spaces had considerable opportunity to exercise control over one another, because suites of laterally connected rooms dominated that component. This plan might indicate extended family or clan-based authority over access to limited portions of the pueblo, although it does not readily support the existence of a supervening authority.

During Component II, roomblocks became more segregated and private, whereas plazas became more integrated and public. To the extent that these altered spatial relations reflect some form of broader, communitywide authority structure, it must have been an authority that either valued or was forced to recognize greater privacy within roomblocks. Perhaps overall group identity and ideology were strengthened through the principle of allowing individual families to be responsible for their own well-being.

Such changes are virtually invisible to most forms of architectural analysis, but the access patterns and integration values of space syntax analysis show a persistent movement toward privately controlled (or at least potentially controllable) and segregated spaces in northern Rio Grande pueblos. It became increasingly difficult for nonresidents to gain access to the deepest and most controlled portions of particular roomblocks. Whether such changes reflect a modification in basic social organization from extended to nuclear families, whether the potential for food shortages resulted in a need for greater control over food supplies, or whether the most private elements of katsina ceremonialism contributed to this change is not entirely clear. In any event, these spatial arrangements permitted individual families or households to have greater control over social interaction and possibly enabled different ethnic or social groups to maintain their own spaces and successfully adapt to life in relatively large and densely populated pueblos with a minimum of social friction.

As part of the same process of architectural change, large, open plazas enclosed by roomblocks became the primary spatial connectors for the community. In one sense, plazas were the built spaces least subject to individual control; in another sense, they were the most controlling spaces. Plazas performed their integrating functions by serving both as stages for communitywide ceremonies and as places where residents could observe their neighbors and be likewise observed. The relatively shallow plaza spaces synchronized with the deeper residential and storage spaces to create a template for ancestral Pueblo settlements that spread throughout the northern Rio Grande and persisted at least until the Spanish *entrada*.

The results of space syntax analysis for Arroyo Hondo and the other sites I have considered inevitably generate additional hypotheses. For example, the increasing differentiation between storage and living spaces that is evident in the Arroyo Hondo Component II and Tijeras Pueblo data suggests that we should ask additional questions about the correlations between specific kinds of rooms and patterns of integration values. Another potential use of space syntax analysis concerns the problem of contemporaneous occupation within pueblos and the need to establish accurate site chronologies. Assuming the availability of data, it might be possible to look at changes in space syntax patterns within large roomblocks or among groups of roomblocks in order to determine construction sequences. This would be particularly useful at sites with long occupation sequences, such as Pecos, San Marcos, Hawikku, and Grasshopper Pueblos.

In another line of future research, a more extensive review of contemporaneous sites in the northern Rio Grande and other parts of the Southwest might test whether the patterns I have observed are local or widespread, ephemeral or persistent. And in more extensive cross-cultural comparisons, consideration should be given to examples of middle-range societies such as tribes, chiefdoms, and their ilk that have occupied a variety of arid regions. For example, the excellent architectural preservation and archaeological records of the Middle East and the Mediterranean region should offer many opportunities for the application of space syntax analysis to a variety of sites (e.g., Banning 1996). Geography is not destiny, but whether any nomothetic generalities exist in the ways in which middle-range societies develop and modify their living spaces is a question waiting to be answered.

What, then, have the arcane diagrams and calculations of space syntax analysis added to our knowledge of Arroyo Hondo Pueblo? On one level, I hope they have convincingly established that diachronic change took place in the manner in which built space was arranged there. My interpretation of that change, based on concepts of social stress, represents a new attempt to answer an old question. If the patterns observed at Arroyo Hondo and the other settlements are found to be replicated in other regions, then space syntax analysis may be an open door to an entirely new way of approaching issues such as social complexity. Even if such patterns are not duplicated in other areas, space syntax analysis will continue to prove a useful method for unraveling particular relationships between social and spatial organization.

On a broader level, I hope this study will encourage a greater use of architectural analysis by archaeologists so that it may "become equivalent to the role now played by the analysis of artifact categories such as chipped stone, pottery, and subsistence remains" (Gilman 1987:560). Through space syntax analysis, one can discern transformations in the arrangement of space, irrespective of whether they are accompanied by other technological or material changes. If cultures leave "architectural fingerprints" as a signature in the archaeological record, then space syntax analysis appears to be an extremely important tool with which archaeologists may identify and learn to read those fingerprints.

Appendix A

The following six tables correspond to the site plans provided in chapter 4 and list the individual integration values associated with each room or other space used in the analysis. The lowest integration and control values are marked with a single asterisk (*), and the highest values are marked with double asterisks (**). The abbreviations used for room function (following Creamer 1993:115) are as follows:

L	Living room (habitation)
S	Storage room
L/S	Living room converted to storage room
L or S	Living or storage room
C	Ceremonial room
CS	Ceremonial storage room
O	Other function
NF	Function indeterminate

ROOMBLOCK *16*, COMPONENT I

Room or Space	Description	Function	Integration Value	Control Value
24	Rooftop	—	1.2023	0.833
24	Second floor	L	1.3947**	0.833
24	First floor	S	1.3562	0.833
26	Rooftop	—	0.9715	1.700
26	First floor	L	1.2552	0.250*

27	Rooftop	—	0.7647	1.500
27	Second floor	L	0.9859	0.667
27	First floor	S	1.2552	1.333
28	Rooftop	—	0.7839	1.417
28	Second floor	L	1.0000	0.583
28	First floor	S	1.1420	0.833
30	Rooftop	—	0.7069	1.200
30	Second floor	L	0.9618	1.333
30	First floor	L/S	1.1253	0.500
31	Rooftop	—	1.2744	0.750
31	Second floor	L	1.1590	1.000
31	First floor	S	0.9618	1.000
32	Rooftop	—	1.0340	2.167★★
32	First floor	S	0.9953	0.250★
33	Rooftop	—	0.7069	1.617
33	Second floor	C	0.9618	0.533
33	First floor	CS	1.1253	1.333
34	Rooftop	—	1.0340	1.583
34	First floor	L	1.2792	0.333
35	Rooftop	—	0.9137	1.700
35	First floor	S	1.1975	0.333
36	Rooftop	—	0.9666	1.500
36	First floor	L	1.0532	1.250
37	Rooftop	—	0.8705	1.700
37	First floor	S	0.7839	0.250★
A	Rooftop	—	0.8410	1.700
A	First floor	—	1.1975	0.333
B	Rooftop	—	0.7434	1.367
B	First floor	—	0.9570	0.583
C	Rooftop	—	0.6800	1.533
C	First floor	—	0.9330	1.033
D	Rooftop	—	0.8320	2.033
D	First floor	—	1.1157	0.250★
E	Rooftop	—	0.9859	1.000
E	First floor	—	1.1734	0.583
F	Rooftop	—	0.8127	1.667
F	Second floor	—	1.0340	0.583
F	First floor	—	1.1590	1.167
G	Rooftop	—	0.6657★	0.833
G	Second floor	—	0.9371	1.000
G	First floor	—	1.2215	0.833
H	Rooftop	—	0.6925	0.950

H	Second floor	—	0.9474	0.833
H	First floor	—	1.1494	0.833
I	Rooftop	—	0.9618	0.750
I	First floor	—	0.8705	0.833
J	Rooftop	—	0.7300	1.250
J	Second floor	—	0.9522	0.833
J	First floor	—	1.1350	1.000
K	Rooftop	—	0.8897	1.667
K	Second floor	—	1.1494	1.333
K	First floor	—	1.3321	0.500
M	Rooftop	—	0.7983	0.833
M	First floor	—	0.9089	1.167
Plaza C	Plaza	—	0.9618	1.667
Plaza D	Plaza	—	1.2071	1.083
Carrier	Outside	—	0.8041	0.583

Average integration value = 1.01

ROOMBLOCK *18*, COMPONENT I

Room or Space	Description	Function	Integration Value	Control Value
5	Rooftop	—	1.0181	1.667
5	Second floor	L	1.0524	0.950
5	First floor	L/S	0.9220	1.833
6	Rooftop	—	1.2752	1.033
6	Second floor	NF	1.3004	0.667
6	First floor	S	1.1183	1.500
7	Rooftop	—	0.9072	1.533
7	Second floor	L	1.0584	0.533
7	First floor	L/S	0.8568	1.000
8	Rooftop	—	0.8619	0.917
8	Second floor	L	1.0282	0.533
8	First floor	S	0.7812	1.334
9	Rooftop	—	0.6250★	1.530
9	Second floor	L	0.8870	0.500
9	First floor	L/S	1.1080	1.083
14	Rooftop	—	1.0736	1.333
14	Second floor	L	1.3508	1.833
14	First floor	L/S	1.5381★★	0.500
32	Rooftop	—	0.9172	1.000

131

32	Second floor	L	0.9828	0.833
32	First floor	S	0.9598	0.625
37	Rooftop	—	0.7560	0.875
37	First floor	L or S	1.0330	0.833
38	Rooftop	—	0.7107	1.333
38	Second floor	L	0.9870	0.750
38	First floor	S	1.2504	1.200
39	Rooftop	—	0.6552	1.833
39	Second floor	L	0.9120	0.533
39	First floor	L/S	1.1590	1.500
42	Rooftop	—	0.8316	1.667
42	Second floor	L	1.0786	0.583
42	First floor	L/S	1.2701	1.167
49	Rooftop	—	0.8660	1.033
49	First floor	S	0.9828	0.833
A	Rooftop	—	0.8518	1.458
A	First floor	—	1.1391	0.333
B	Rooftop	—	0.8410	1.000
B	First floor	—	0.9324	0.583
C	Rooftop	—	1.0534	0.583
C	First floor	—	1.1744	1.167
D	Rooftop	—	0.8316	1.033
D	Second floor	—	1.0786	0.533
D	First floor	—	1.2701	0.833
F	Rooftop	—	0.6855	1.400
F	First floor	—	0.9728	0.333
H	Rooftop	—	1.1375	1.000
H	Second floor	—	1.4073	1.333
H	First floor	—	1.6861	0.500
I	Rooftop	—	0.9224	0.833
I	Second floor	—	1.1794	1.000
I	First floor	—	1.4264	0.833
M	Rooftop	—	0.8820	1.325
M	First floor	—	1.1693	0.333
N	Rooftop	—	0.9375	0.625
N	First floor	—	1.0937	0.625
O	Rooftop	—	0.9929	1.533
O	First floor	—	1.0786	0.500
P	Rooftop	—	0.8669	1.450
P	First floor	—	1.1540	0.333
Plaza G	Plaza	—	0.6905	3.700★★
Plaza I	Plaza	—	0.6703	1.458

Plaza J	Plaza	—	0.8417	1.325
Kiva G–5	Ceremonial	C	0.9778	0.125★
Carrier	Outside	—	1.1290	0.333

Average integration value = 1.02

ROOMBLOCK 5–6, COMPONENT I

Room or Space	Description	Function	Integration Value	Control Value
5	Rooftop	—	0.7035	1.250
5	Second floor	L	0.9470	0.700
5	First floor	L/S	1.0958	0.750
6	Rooftop	—	0.9876	1.283
6	Second floor	L	1.2717	0.750
6	First floor	O	1.5555	1.000
7	Rooftop	—	0.7373	1.200
7	Second floor	L	0.9538	0.500
7	First floor	L/S	1.0350	1.667
8	Rooftop	—	0.8456	1.333
8	Second floor	L	1.0620	0.500
8	First floor	L/S	1.0891	1.917
9	Rooftop	—	0.7509	0.900
9	Second floor	L	0.9606	0.667
9	First floor	L/S	1.0282	0.950
10	Rooftop	—	0.8456	1.083
10	First floor	S	1.0485	1.000
11	Rooftop	—	0.8320	1.333
11	Second floor	C	1.0891	0.750
11	First floor	CS	1.2244	0.833
12	Rooftop	—	0.9876	0.917
12	First floor	L or S	1.1432	1.083
13	Rooftop	—	1.0079	1.167
13	First floor	L or S	1.1635	0.667
14	Rooftop	—	0.7103	1.667
14	Second floor	S	0.9335	0.400
14	First floor	L/S	0.9876	1.917★★
A	Rooftop	—	0.9132	1.917★★
A	First floor	—	1.2244	0.250★
B	Rooftop	—	1.0079	1.500
B	First floor	—	1.3190	0.333

C	Rooftop	—	0.9200	1.700
C	First floor	—	1.2311	0.250★
D	Rooftop	—	0.8456	1.400
D	First floor	—	1.1567	0.333
E	Rooftop	—	0.8117	1.450
E	First floor	—	1.1228	0.333
F	Rooftop	—	0.6967★	1.283
F	First floor	—	0.9267	0.458
G	Rooftop	—	0.8388	1.283
G	Second floor	—	1.1364	1.250
G	First floor	—	1.4476	0.500
H	Rooftop	—	1.0214	1.000
H	Second floor	—	1.3055	0.833
H	First floor	—	1.5897★★	1.000
Plaza K	Plaza	—	0.9731	1.667
Plaza L	Plaza	—	0.9438	0.583
Carrier	Outside	—	1.0079	0.533

Average integration value = 1.02

ROOMBLOCK *16*, COMPONENT II

Room or Space	Description	Function	Integration Value	Control Value
1	Rooftop	—	0.7476	1.458
1	First floor	L	1.0433	0.583
4	Rooftop	—	1.3390	1.333
4	First floor	L	1.6676	0.500
5	Rooftop	—	0.9611	1.000
5	First floor	L or S	1.2240	0.667
6	Rooftop	—	1.2733	1.333
6	First floor	L	1.6019	0.500
9	Rooftop	—	1.0261	1.750
9	First floor	S	1.3550	0.333
10	Rooftop	—	1.2076	1.500
10	First floor	S	1.5197	0.833
11	Rooftop	—	0.9447	1.125
11	First floor	L	1.2733	0.500
13	Rooftop	—	1.6033	1.500
13	First floor	S	1.8155	0.833
14	Rooftop	—	1.4869	1.333

14	First floor	L	1.7991	0.833
15	Rooftop	—	1.7991	1.333
15	First floor	S	2.1276★★	0.500
17	Rooftop	—	1.4705	1.000
17	First floor	L	1.7826	1.000
18	Rooftop	—	1.8155	0.833
18	First floor	L	2.1276★★	1.000
19	Rooftop	—	1.1583	1.333
19	First floor	L	1.4705	0.833
20	Rooftop	—	0.8790	1.625
20	First floor	L	1.2070	0.333
21	Rooftop	—	0.7476	1.292
21	First floor	L	1.0597	1.000
22	Rooftop	—	0.9611	1.083
22	First floor	S	1.2733	0.833
38	Rooftop	—	0.9447	1.625
38	First floor	S	1.2733	0.500
A	Rooftop	—	1.0269	1.000
A	First floor	—	1.3222	1.000
B	Rooftop	—	1.3390	0.833
B	First floor	—	1.6348	0.833
Plaza C	Plaza	—	0.6325★	4.083★★
Plaza D	Plaza	—	0.9529	0.625
Kiva C	Ceremonial	C	0.9611	0.125★
Carrier	Outside	—	0.9529	0.625

Average integration value = 1.30

ROOMBLOCK *9*, COMPONENT II

Room or Space	Description	Function	Integration Value	Control Value
6	Rooftop	—	1.1333	1.667
6	First floor	S	1.5777	0.500
8	Rooftop	—	1.4444	0.833
8	First floor	S	1.8444★★	1.000
9	Rooftop	—	1.4444	0.833
9	First floor	L or S	1.8000	0.833
10	Rooftop	—	0.8222	1.643
10	First floor	L	1.2666	0.333
11	Rooftop	—	0.8222	1.643

11	First floor	L	1.2666	0.333
12	Rooftop	—	0.7333	0.976
12	First floor	L	1.0881	0.667
13	Rooftop	—	1.0444	1.333
13	First floor	L	1.4000	1.333
A	Rooftop	—	0.7333	1.476
A	First floor	—	1.1777	0.333
B	Rooftop	—	1.0444	1.500
B	First floor	—	1.4444	0.833
Plaza C	Plaza	—	0.5111★	3.500★★
Plaza F	Plaza	—	0.9333	0.643
Kiva C	Ceremonial	C	0.9555	0.143★
Carrier	Outside	—	0.9333	0.643

Average integration value = 1.16

ROOMBLOCK *10,* COMPONENT II

Room or Space	Description	Function	Integration Value	Control Value
3	Rooftop	—	1.1548	1.250
3	First floor	L	1.7596★★	0.500
4	First floor	L	1.5947	0.333
5	Rooftop	—	0.6599	2.333
5	First floor	L or S	1.2647	0.250★
6	Rooftop	—	0.6049★	0.917
6	First floor	L	0.9898	2.333
A	First floor	—	1.1760	0.333
B	Rooftop	—	1.1548	1.250
B	First floor	—	1.7596★★	0.500
Plaza C	Plaza	—	0.9898	2.333★★
Kiva C	Ceremonial	C	1.5947	0.333
Carrier	Outside	—	1.5947	0.333

Average integration value = 1.2859

Appendix B

ROOMBLOCK DATA FOR TIJERAS PUEBLO (LA 581)

The source of the following data is Blevins and Atwood 1974. Rooms for which no data were available are marked with an asterisk (*).

ROOMBLOCK 3

Room No.	Doorway(s)	Second Floor	Third Floor	Classification
52*	—	—	—	—
53	—	—	—	Habitation
54*	—	—	—	—
55	—	—	—	Storage?
56	South wall	—	—	Storage
57	North wall	—	—	Habitation
58	—	—	—	Storage
59*	—	—	—	—
60	North wall	—	—	Storage
61*	—	—	—	—
62	South wall	—	—	Storage
63	North wall	—	+	Storage
64	—	—	—	Kiva
65*	—	—	—	—
66	East wall	—	—	Habitation
107*	—	—	—	—

ROOMBLOCK 4

Room No.	Doorway(s)	Second Floor	Third Floor	Classification
1	West wall	+	—	Habitation
2	East wall	+	—	Habitation/storage
15	—	—	—	Habitation/storage
16	—	—	—	Habitation
27★	—	—	—	—
28	—	—	—	Storage
31	—	—	—	Storage
32	—	—	—	Storage
33	—	—	—	Storage
67★	—	—	—	—
68	—	—	—	Habitation
69	North & east walls	—	—	Habitation
70	—	+	—	Habitation
71★	—	—	—	—
72	—	—	—	Storage
73	North & east walls	+	—	Storage/Habitation
74★	—	—	—	—
75★	—	—	—	—
76★	—	—	—	—
77★	—	—	—	—
78★	—	—	—	—

ROOMBLOCK 5

Room No.	Doorway(s)	Second Floor	Third Floor	Classification
3	—	—	—	?
6	—	—	—	Ceremonial
9	West wall	+	+	Habitation
10	—	+	+	Habitation/food process
14	East wall, 2 floors	+	+	Habitation/ceremonial
25	South wall	—	—	Utility/food processing?
26	—	—	—	Ceremonial
79	West wall	—	—	Storage
80★	—	—	—	—

81	—	—	—	Habitation
82	—	—	—	Habitation
83★	—	—	—	—
85	South wall	—	—	Habitation
86★	—	—	—	—
87★	—	—	—	—
88	—	—	—	Storage?
89	North & east walls	—	—	Storage/specialized activity
90	West wall	—	—	Storage
91★	—	—	—	—
92	—	—	—	Specialized activity
93★	—	—	—	—
94★	—	—	—	—
95★	—	—	—	—

ROOMBLOCK 2 (PARTIAL LISTING)

Room No.	Doorway(s)	Second Floor	Third Floor	Classification
7	—	+	+	?
8	—	+	+	?
17	East & west walls	+	—	Habitation/storage
51	South wall	—	—	Storage
96	East wall	—	—	Habitation
102★	—	—	—	—

Appendix C

INTEGRATION AND CONTROL VALUES FOR TIJERAS PUEBLO

In the following table, the lowest integration and control values are marked with a single asterisk (★), and the highest values are marked with double asterisks (★★).

Room or Space	Description	Integration Value	Control Value
1	Rooftop	1.0530	1.033
1	Second floor	0.9529	0.833
1	First floor	1.1410	0.833
2	Rooftop	1.2291	1.333
2	Second floor	1.3853	0.667
2	First floor	1.3793	1.333
6	Rooftop	1.0510	0.833
6	First floor	1.3712	1.000
7	Rooftop	0.7747	0.916
7	Third floor	0.9949	0.833
7	Second floor	1.2191	1.500
7	First floor	1.4473	0.500
8	Rooftop	0.9028	1.666
8	Third floor	1.2110	0.833
8	Second floor	1.3132	1.000
8	First floor	1.4193	0.500
9	Rooftop	0.8448	1.016
9	Third floor	1.0650	0.833
9	Second floor	1.2852	1.000

9	First floor	1.4914	1.000
10	Rooftop	0.8308	1.083
10	Third floor	1.0229	0.833
10	Second floor	1.2091	1.000
10	First floor	1.3853	0.833
14	Rooftop	1.0410	1.000
14	Third floor	1.2431	0.833
14	Second floor	1.2491	1.833
14	First floor	1.4774	0.333
17	Rooftop	1.0269	1.083
17	Second floor	1.2271	0.667
17	First floor	1.3572	1.333
32	Rooftop	1.3072	1.033
32	Second floor	1.2872	1.333
32	First floor	1.1054	0.500
33	Rooftop	1.1831	1.667
33	First floor	1.5354	0.333
51	Rooftop	1.4994	1.250
51	First floor	1.7190	1.000
53	Rooftop	1.5074	1.250
53	First floor	1.7356	0.500
54	Rooftop	1.2832	1.333
54	First floor	1.5034	0.580
55	Rooftop	1.6074	2.083
55	First floor	1.5114	0.250
56	Rooftop	1.4133	1.083
56	First floor	1.5375	0.833
57	Rooftop	1.2852	1.167
57	First floor	1.5099	0.833
58	Rooftop	1.2852	1.833
58	First floor	1.4133	0.333
59	Rooftop	1.1430	1.000
59	First floor	1.3032	1.083
60	Rooftop	1.4333	1.083
60	First floor	1.3172	0.667
61	Rooftop	1.3052	1.667
61	First floor	1.6334	0.333
62	Rooftop	1.1611	1.033
62	First floor	1.3883	0.833
63	Rooftop	0.9829	1.700
63	Second floor	1.2051	0.700
63	First floor	1.4053	1.000

64	Kiva rooftop	0.8708	1.083
64	Kiva	1.0990	0.500
66	Rooftop	0.8908	1.033
66	First floor	0.7987	0.416
67	Rooftop	1.2211	1.200
67	First floor	1.4493	0.500
68	Rooftop	0.9969	2.416
68	First floor	1.2211	0.200★
69	Rooftop	0.8968	0.950
69	First floor	0.8127	0.416
70	Rooftop	1.1390	1.250
70	Second floor	1.3632	1.333
70	First floor	1.5915	0.500
71	Rooftop	0.9268	2.000
71	First floor	1.1470	0.250
72	Rooftop	0.8027	1.583
72	First floor	1.0309	0.250
73	Rooftop	0.8208	0.833
73	Second floor	1.0109	0.833
73	First floor	1.1390	1.016
74	Rooftop	1.0009	2.016
74	First floor	1.2291	0.250
75	Rooftop	1.1831	1.583
75	First floor	1.4113	0.333
76	Rooftop	1.3592	1.333
76	First floor	1.5875	0.500
77	Rooftop	0.9048	1.833
77	First floor	1.1290	0.700
78	Rooftop	0.7987	1.283
78	First floor	1.9269	0.333
79	Rooftop	1.0850	1.167
79	First floor	1.3092	0.833
80	Rooftop	1.3152	1.833
80	First floor	1.0870	0.250
81	Rooftop	0.9484	1.833
81	First floor	1.1771	0.250
82	Rooftop	0.8087	1.333
82	First floor	1.0369	0.333
85	Rooftop	1.0830	1.167
85	First floor	1.2571	0.833
89	Rooftop	1.2311	1.250
89	First floor	1.2331	1.033

90	Rooftop	1.3793	1.067
90	First floor	1.5614	0.667
91	Rooftop	1.5714	1.667
91	First floor	1.7996	0.333
92	Rooftop	1.7556	1.667
92	First floor	1.9838★★	0.333
96	Rooftop	1.7236	0.833
96	First floor	1.9438	1.000
A	Rooftop	1.5414	1.833
A	First floor	1.7696	0.333
Plaza	Plaza	0.6466★	5.000★★
Carrier	Outside	0.8748	0.083

Mean integration value = 1.2465

Notes

Chapter 3. Arroyo Hondo Pueblo in the Context of Cultural Change

1. Sapawe Pueblo, located in the Chama Valley of northern New Mexico, is believed to have contained as many as 4,400 rooms grouped around seven large plazas (Morgan 1994:215–216).

2. Building with puddled adobe involves piling up a series of courses by hand, each approximately 1 meter in height, and letting each dry before adding the next course. It was one of the basic construction methods used during the Coalition and early Classic periods (Creamer 1993:16). A number of contemporaneous pueblos, including Poshuouinge, Pindi, Sapawe, and Pot Creek, display the same basic construction techniques.

3. Nels Nelson (1914) noted the presence of 10 doorways among the 110 rooms he excavated at Arroyo Hondo Pueblo. Despite his recognition of a sequential occupation there, his notes do not indicate which rooms could properly be assigned to Component I or II. Therefore, none of these materials were incorporated into the present study.

Chapter 4. A Primer on Space Syntax Analysis

1. Topology is the mathematical study of position and is closely linked to the mathematical field of graph theory. It is concerned with the properties of geometric forms that do not vary even when the forms are transformed, such as changes in size, shape, or orientation.

2. The carrier space is defined as the surrounding, undefined, and undifferentiated open space that "carries" a building or settlement. The term *root* was first used by the British mathematician Arthur Cawley (1821–1895) in connection with the designation of a starting point for a network graph. (See Biggs, Lloyd, and Wilson 1976.)

3. Although Hillier and Hanson (1984:112) produced a table of numbers called "D values" that can be used to hand-calculate integration values, I utilized a computer software package developed at the Bartlett School of Graduate Studies, University College London, London WC1E 6BT, U.K. (Dalton 1991). The software is

distributed at no charge to bona fide researchers. Interested persons can contact Professor Bill Hillier at the above address or via the Internet at B.hillier@vel.ac.uk. The space syntax website can be viewed at http://doric.bart.vel.ac.uk/web/spacesyntax.

Chapter 5. A Space Syntax Analysis of Arroyo Hondo Pueblo

1. The six roomblocks I analyzed were those in which the greatest number of contiguous rooms had been excavated for each component. The numbers of excavated rooms vary but represent the best data set available from the Arroyo Hondo "universe."

2. Readers may question my incorporation of unexcavated rooms into the analysis. The original research design at Arroyo Hondo was not developed with space syntax analysis in mind, and excavation was directed toward numerous small groups of rooms rather than extensive groups of contiguous rooms within each roomblock. In some situations, rooms that were otherwise unexcavated revealed door or vent connections with excavated rooms, thereby strongly suggesting at least a potential association. In other cases, one or more unexcavated rooms were located between plazas and groups of contiguous, excavated rooms. In these limited situations, a few unexcavated rooms were incorporated into the justified access graphs to provide a more complete picture of potential accessibility with the roomblocks.

3. Not every excavated room in roomblock 16 is accounted for in this diagram, because, for example, rooms 8 and 38 revealed no apparent connections to the mass of rooms in the center of the roomblock. I used a similar approach for other roomblocks in which complete relationships between rooms could not be determined.

4. A complete list of the integration and control values derived for the spaces depicted on the justified access diagrams is provided in Appendix A.

5. Room 22 is the only room fronting plaza C that was identified as a storage room in Component II roomblock 16. Room 19 is the only living room located in the second row of storage rooms.

6. Creamer (1993:115) identified room 9 in roomblock 9 as either a living or a storage room, but Beal (n.d.) considered it to have been a storage room. For the purposes of this study, I treated it as a storage room.

7. None of the excavated Component·II rooms was classified as "living converted to storage," "ceremonial," or "ceremonial storage."

8. In Component I roomblock 16, the second-story rooftop above a ceremonial room (33) had the second lowest integration value (0.6925) in the roomblock, and it was not substantially greater than the lowest value (0.6841). The inference is that spaces associated with access to this ceremonial room were also highly integrative spaces, although for reasons already mentioned, the associated storage room has a higher and more segregating value.

Chapter 6. Interpretations and Comparisons

1. The time period being analyzed is important because a number of unique attributes, such as painted kiva walls, were specifically associated with the earlier

(1300–1313 C.E.) occupation at Tijeras Pueblo. Such factors, when coupled with practical problems of assigning initial construction dates to a number of rooms, justify the limited focus on the latest occupation.

2. As in the case of Arroyo Hondo, the residents of Tijeras constructed a great kiva at some distance from the main portion of the pueblo.

3. Statistical comparison between Arroyo Hondo and Tijeras Pueblos using the Student's T-test at the 95 percent level of confidence indicates that Tijeras and Arroyo Hondo Component I represent different populations whereas Tijeras and Component II represent the same population.

4. The Museum of New Mexico in Santa Fe retains a series of excavation notes, together with a rough map of the East House excavations of 1910, but this information was less comprehensive than that for the South House and was not used in this analysis.

5. Of course, my analysis of Acoma Pueblo is based on twentieth-century architectural data rather than on 500 years of architectural history. But even this limited data set supports the argument that the Acoma people continued a long Puebloan tradition of organizing built space in a discernible and predictable manner.

6. *Calpulli* were a type of tribal organization that evolved into territorially based corporate social units controlled by a noble. Each Aztec was born into and retained service obligations to one of these land-owning, tax-paying units (Smith 1993:198-199; Weaver 1993:468). Although calpulli were located throughout the countryside, individual wards or barrios of the Aztec capitol, Tenochtitlan, were associated with specific calpulli. *Ayllus* were similar to calpulli in the sense that they were kinship- and territory-based social units led by a noble. Although ayllus had a long history in the Andean highlands, they were incorporated into the fabric of the Inka empire, and each *ayllu* was associated with a particular sector or barrio in the Inka capitol, Cuzco (Hyslop 1990; Richardson 1994).

7. Tijeras Pueblo appears to have been transitional in this regard. There, a large, square kiva had two sides incorporated into a roomblock and two sides bordering the plaza (see fig. 6.1, room 64). Similar square kivas are seen at Paa-ko, several miles to the north of Tijeras (Lambert 1954).

References

Adams, E. C.

1989   Changing Form and Function in Western Pueblo Ceremonial Architecture from A.D. 1000 to A.D. 1500. In *The Architecture of Social Integration in Prehistoric Pueblos*, edited by W. D. Lipe and M. Hegmon, pp. 155–160. Crow Canyon Archaeological Center, Cortez, Colorado.

1991   *The Origin and Development of the Pueblo Katsina Cult.* University of Arizona Press, Tucson.

1996   The Pueblo III–Pueblo IV Transition in the Hopi Area, Arizona. In *The Prehistoric Pueblo World A.D. 1150–1350*, edited by M. Adler, pp. 48–58. University of Arizona Press, Tucson

Ahlstrom, R. V. N, C. Van West, and J. S. Dean

1995   Environmental and Chronological Factors in the Mesa Verde: Northern Rio Grande Migration. *Journal of Anthropological Archaeology* 14(2):125–142.

Altman, I., and M. M. Chemers

1980   Cultural Aspects of Environment-Behavior Relationships. In *Handbook of Cross-Cultural Psychology*, vol. 5, *Social Psychology*, edited by H. C. Triandis and R. W. Brislin, pp. 335–393. Allyn and Bacon, Boston.

149

Anella, T.
1992   Learning from the Pueblos. In *Pueblo Style and Regional Architecture*, edited by N. Markovich, W. F. E. Preiser, and F. Sturm. Van Nostrand Reinhold, New York.

Ankerl, G.
1981   *Experimental Sociology of Architecture*. Mouton, The Hague.

Arnheim, R.
1995   A Study in Spatial Counterpoint. In *Poetics of Space*, edited by S. Yates, pp. 7–22. University of New Mexico Press, Albuquerque.

Bandelier, A.
1971   *The Delight Makers*. Harcourt Brace, San Diego.
[1890]

Banning, E. B.
1996   Houses, Compounds, and Mansions in the Prehistoric Near East. In *People Who Lived in Big Houses: Archaeological Perspectives on Large Domestic Structures*, edited by G. Coupland and E. B. Banning, pp. 165–185. Monographs in World Archaeology no. 27. Prehistory Press, Madison, Wisconsin.

Basso, K. H.
1996   *Wisdom Sits in Places: Landscape and Language among the Western Apache*. University of New Mexico Press, Albuquerque.

Beach, M. A., and C. S. Causey
1984   Bone Artifacts from Arroyo Hondo Pueblo. Additional Report I in *The Faunal Remains from Arroyo Hondo, New Mexico: A Study in Short-term Subsistence Change*, by R. W. Lang and A. H. Harris. Arroyo Hondo Archaeological Series, vol. 5. School of American Research Press, Santa Fe, New Mexico.

Beal, J. D.
1971   Arroyo Hondo Architectural Report 1971. Unpublished manu-script. School of American Research, Santa Fe, New Mexico.
1972   Report on Arroyo Hondo Architecture 1972. Unpublished manu-script. School of American Research, Santa Fe, New Mexico.
n.d.   Overview of Arroyo Hondo Architecture. Unpublished manuscript. School of American Research, Santa Fe, New Mexico.

Bell, P., J. Fisher, and R. Loomia
1978   *Environmental Psychology*. W. B. Saunders, Philadelphia.

Bernardini, W.

1996   Conflict, Migration, and the Social Environment: Interpreting Architectural Change in Early and Late Pueblo IV Aggregations. Paper presented at the 61st annual meeting of the Society for American Archaeology, New Orleans.

Biggs, N. L., E. K. Lloyd, and R. L. Wilson

1976   *Graph Theory 1736–1936.* Clarendon Press, Oxford.

Blanton, R. E.

1994   *Houses and Households: A Comparative Study.* Plenum, New York.

Blevins, B. B., and W. L. Atwood

1974   Appendix to Preliminary Report of Tijeras Pueblo: Summary of All Excavated Rooms. Unpublished manuscript. Maxwell Museum, University of New Mexico, Albuquerque.

Bohrer, V. L.

1986   The Ethnobotanical Pollen Record at Arroyo Hondo Pueblo. Additional Report I in *Food, Diet, and Population at Prehistoric Arroyo Hondo Pueblo, New Mexico,* by W. Wetterstrom. Arroyo Hondo Archaeological Series, vol. 6. School of American Research Press, Santa Fe, New Mexico.

Bonanno, A., T. Gouder, C. Malone, and S. Stoddart

1990a   Monuments in an Island Society: The Maltese Context. *World Archaeology* 22(2):189–205.

1990b   *The Logic of Practice.* Stanford University Press, Stanford, California.

Bradley, B.

1993   Planning, Growth, and Functional Differentiation at a Prehistoric Pueblo: A Case Study from Southwest Colorado. *Journal of Field Archaeology* 20:23–42.

Brandt, E. A.

1994   Egalitarianism, Hierarchy, and Centralization in the Pueblos. In *The Ancient Southwest Community,* edited by W. H. Wills and R. D. Leonard, pp. 103–118. University of New Mexico Press, Albuquerque.

Brody, J. J.

1991   *Anasazi and Pueblo Painting.* University of New Mexico Press, Albuquerque.

Brown, F.

1990a Comment on Chapman: Some Cautionary Notes on the Application of Spatial Measures to Prehistoric Settlements. In *The Social Archaeology of Houses*, edited by R. Samson, pp. 93–109. Edinburgh University Press, Edinburgh.

1990b Analyzing Small Building Plans: A Morphological Approach. In *The Social Archaeology of Houses*, edited by R. Samson, pp. 259–276. Edinburgh University Press, Edinburgh.

Brown, F. E., and J. P. Steadman

1991 The Morphology of British Housing: An Empirical Basis for Policy and Research. *Environment and Planning B: Planning and Design* 18:385–415.

Bullock, P.

1993 Lords of the Southwest. Paper presented at the Fifth Occasional Anasazi Symposium, Farmington, New Mexico.

Bustard, W.

1995 Genotypes of Space: A Spatial Analysis of Domestic Structures in Chaco Canyon. Paper presented at the 60th annual meeting of the Society for American Archaeology, Minneapolis.

1996 Space as Place: Small and Great House Spatial Organization in Chaco Canyon, New Mexico, A.D. 1000–1150. Ph.D. dissertation, University of New Mexico, Albuquerque.

2003 Pueblo Bonito: When a House Is Not a Home. In *Pueblo Bonito: Center of the Chacoan World*, edited by Jill E. Neitzel, pp. 80–93. Smithsonian Books, Washington, D.C.

Cameron, C. M.

1995 Migration and the Movement of Southwestern Peoples. *Journal of Anthropological Archaeology* 14(2):104–124.

Carnap, R.

1995 Space. In *Poetics of Space: A Critical Photographic Anthology*, edited by S. Yates, pp. 77–83. University of New Mexico Press, Albuquerque.

Castri, J.

1979 *Connectivity, Complexity, and Catastrophe in Large-Scale Systems*. John Wiley and Sons, Chichester, England.

Chapman, J.

1990 Social Inequality on Bulgarian Tells and the Varna Problem. In *The Social Archaeology of Houses*, edited by R. Samson, pp. 49–92. Edinburgh University Press, Edinburgh.

Chippendale, C.

1992 Grammars of Archaeological Design: A Generative and Geometric Approach to the Form of Artifacts. In *Representations in Archaeology*, edited by J. C. Gardin and C. S. Peebles, pp. 251–276. Indiana University Press, Bloomington.

Clark, J.

1995 Domestic Architecture in the Early Classic Period. In *The Roosevelt Community Development Study: New Perspectives in Tonto Prehistory*, edited by M. D. Elson, M. T. Stark, and D. A. Gregory, pp. 251–305. Anthropological Papers no. 15. Center for Desert Archaeology, Tucson.

Cooper, L.

1995 Space Syntax Analysis of Chacoan Great Houses. Ph.D. dissertation, University of Arizona, Tucson.

Cordell, L. S.

1975 *The 1974 Excavation of Tijeras Pueblo, Cibola National Forest, New Mexico*. Report no. 5. USDA Forest Service, Southwest Region, Albuquerque.

1977a *The 1975 Excavation of Tijeras Pueblo, Cibola National Forest, New Mexico*. Report no. 18. USDA Forest Service, Southwest Region, Albuquerque.

1977b *The 1976 Excavation of Tijeras Pueblo, Cibola National Forest, New Mexico*. Report no. 18. USDA Forest Service, Southwest Region. Albuquerque.

1980 *Tijeras Canyon: Analyses of the Past*. University of New Mexico Press, Albuquerque.

1984 *Prehistory of the Southwest*. Academic Press, New York.

1989a Prehistory: Eastern Anasazi. In *Handbook of North American Indians*, vol. 9, *Southwest,* edited by A. Ortiz, pp. 113–151. Smithsonian Institution Press, Washington, D.C.

1989b Northern and Central Rio Grande. In *Dynamics of Southwest Prehistory*, edited by L. S. Cordell and G. Gumerman, pp. 293–336. Smithsonian Institution Press, Washington, D.C.

1995 Tracing Migration Pathways from the Receiving End. *Journal of Anthropological Archaeology* 14(2):203–211.

1996 Big Sites, Big Questions: Pueblos in Transition. In *The Prehistoric Pueblo World A.D. 1150–1350*, edited by M. Adler, pp. 228–240. University of Arizona Press, Tucson.

Cordell, L. S., ed.

1980   *Tijeras Canyon: Analyses of the Past.* University of New Mexico Press, Albuquerque.

Cordell, L., D. Doyel, and K. Kintigh

1994   Processes of Aggregation in the Prehistoric Southwest. In *Themes in Southwest Prehistory*, edited by G. Gumerman, pp. 109–133. School of American Research Press, Santa Fe, New Mexico.

Creamer, W.

1993   *The Architecture of Arroyo Hondo Pueblo New Mexico.* School of American Research Press, Santa Fe, New Mexico.

Crown, P.

1994   *Ceramics and Ideology: Salado Polychrome Pottery.* University of New Mexico Press, Albuquerque.

Crown, P. L., and T. A. Kohler

1990   Community Dynamics, Site Structure, and Aggregation in the Northern Rio Grande. In *The Ancient Southwestern Community*, edited by W. H. Wills and R. D. Leonard, pp. 103–117. University of New Mexico Press, Albuquerque.

Crown, P. L., J. D. Orcutt, and T. A. Kohler

1996   Pueblo Culture in Transition: The Northern Rio Grande. In *The Prehistoric Pueblo World A.D. 1150–1350*, edited by M. Adler, pp. 188–204. University of Arizona Press, Tucson.

Dalton, N. S.

1991   *An Advanced Tutorial on Axman.* Bartlett School of Architecture and Planning, London.

Dean, J. S.

1996   Kayenta Anasazi Settlement Transformations in Northeastern Arizona A.D. 1150 to 1350. In *The Prehistoric Pueblo World A.D. 1150–1350*, edited by M. Adler, pp. 29–47. University of Arizona Press, Tucson.

Dickson, D. B., Jr.

1975   Settlement Pattern Stability and Change in the Middle Northern Rio Grande Region, New Mexico: A Test of Some Hypotheses. *American Antiquity* 40(2):159–171.

1979   *Prehistoric Pueblo Settlement Patterns: The Arroyo Hondo, New Mexico, Site Survey.* School of American Research Press, Santa Fe, New Mexico.

Dohm, K. M.

1990   Effect of Population Nucleation on House Size for Pueblos in the American Southwest. *Journal of Anthropological Archaeology* 9(3):201–239.

1996   Rooftop Zuni: Extending Household Territory beyond Apartment Walls. In *People Who Lived in Big Houses: Archaeological Perspectives on Large Domestic Structures*, edited by G. Coupland and E. B. Banning, pp. 89–106. Monographs in World Archaeology no. 27, Madison, Wisconsin.

Douglas, M.

1991   The Idea of a Home: A Kind of Space. *Social Research* 58(1):287–307.

Draper, P.

1973   Crowding among Hunter-Gatherers: The !Kung Bushmen. *Science* 182:301–303.

Durkheim, E.

1964   *The Division of Labor in Society*. Free Press, New York.
[1893]

Egenter, N.

1992a   Introduction: Micro- and Macrotheories. In *Architectural Anthropology*, vol. 1, edited by N. Egenter, pp. 19–88. Structure Mundi, Lausanne, Switzerland.

1992b   Architectural Anthropology: Outlines of a Constructive Human Past. In *Architectural Anthropology*, vol. 1, edited by N. Egenter, pp. 145–171. Structura Mundi, Lausanne, Switzerland.

Evans, G. W., S. J. Lepore, and A. Schroeder

1996   The Role of Interior Design Elements in Human Responses to Crowding. *Journal of Personality and Social Psychology* 70(1):41–46.

Fairclough, G.

1992   Meaningful Constructions: Spatial and Functional Analysis of Medieval Buildings. *Antiquity* 66:348–366.

Fangmeier, K. L.

1998   A Pattern Recognition Analysis of Household Space and Activities in Two Pueblo Communities: Issues in Theory, Method, and Interpretation. Paper presented at the 63d annual meeting of the Society for American Archaeology, Seattle.

Ferguson, T. J.
1993   Historic Zuni Architecture and Society: A Structural Analysis. Ph.D. dissertation, University of New Mexico, Albuquerque.
1996   *Historic Zuni Architecture and Society.* University of Arizona Press, Tucson.
2002   Dowa Yalanne: The Architecture of Zuni Resistance and Social Change during the Pueblo Revolt. In *Archaeologies of the Pueblo Revolt*, edited by R. Preucel, pp. 33–44. University of New Mexico Press, Albuquerque.

Foster, S.
1989   Analysis of Spatial Patterns in Buildings (Access Analysis) as an Insight into Social Structure: Examples from the Scottish Atlantic Iron Age. *Antiquity* 63:40–50.

Fried, M. H.
1967   *The Evolution of Political Society: An Essay in Political Anthropology.* Random House, New York.

Gilman, P.
1987   Architecture as Artifact: Pit Structures and Pueblos in the American Southwest. *American Antiquity* 52(3):538–564.

Greenbie, B. B.
1974   Social Territory, Community Health, and Urban Planning. *Journal of the American Institute of Planners* 40(2):74–82.

Gumerman, G. J., and J. S. Dean
1989   Prehistoric Cooperation and Competition in the Western Anasazi Area. In *Dynamics of Southwestern Prehistory*, edited by L. Cordell and G. J. Gumerman, pp. 99–148. Smithsonian Institution Press, Washington, D.C.

Gutman, R.
1972   *People and Buildings.* Basic Books, New York.

Haas, J.
1990   Warfare and the Evolution of Tribal Polities in the Prehistoric Southwest. In *The Anthropology of War*, edited by J. Haas, pp. 171–189. Cambridge University Press, Cambridge.

Haas, J., and W. Creamer
1996   The Role of Warfare in the Pueblo III Period. In *The Prehistoric Pueblo World A.D. 1150–1350,* edited by M. Adler, pp. 205–213. University of Arizona Press, Tucson.

156

Habicht-Mauche, J.
1993   *The Pottery from Arroyo Hondo Pueblo, New Mexico: Tribalization and Trade in the Northern Rio Grande.* School of American Research Press, Santa Fe, New Mexico.
1995   Changing Patterns of Pottery Manufacture and Trade in the Northern Rio Grande Region. In *Ceramic Production in the American Southwest*, edited by B. J. Mills and P. L. Crown, pp. 167–199. University of Arizona Press, Tucson.

Hage, P., and F. Harary
1983   *Structural Models in Anthropology.* Cambridge University Press, Cambridge.

Hall, E. T.
1966   *The Hidden Dimension.* Doubleday, Garden City, New York.

Hanson, J.
1998   *Decoding Homes and Houses.* Cambridge University Press, Cambridge.

Hays, K. A.
1993   When Is a Symbol Archaeologically Meaningful? Meaning, Function, and Prehistoric Visual Arts. In *Archaeological Theory: Who Sets the Agenda?* edited by N. Yoffee and A. Sherratt, pp. 81–92. Cambridge University Press, Cambridge.

Hegmon, M.
1996   Variability in Food Production, Strategies of Storage and Sharing, and the Pithouse-to-Pueblo Transition in the Northern Southwest. In *Evolving Complexity and Environmental Risk in the Prehistoric Southwest,* edited by J. A. Tainter and B. B. Tainter, pp. 223–250. Santa Fe Institute Studies in the Sciences of Complexity, vol. 24. Addison-Wesley, Reading, Pennsylvania.

Herr, S., and J. L. Clark
1997   Patterns in the Pathways: Early Historic Migrations in the Rio Grande Pueblos. *Kiva* 62(4):364–389.

Hewett, E. L.
1938   *Parajito Plateau and Its Ancient People.* University of New Mexico Press, Albuquerque.

Hieb, L. H.
1992   The Metaphors of Hopi Architectural Experience in Comparative
        Perspective. In *Pueblo Style and Regional Architecture*, edited by
        N. Markovich, W. F. E. Preiser, and F. Sturm, pp. 122–132.
        Van Nostrand Reinhold, New York.

Hill, J.
1970   *Broken K Pueblo: Prehistoric Social Organization in the American
        Southwest.* University of Arizona Press, Tucson.

Hill, W. W.
1982   *Ethnography of Santa Clara Pueblo.* Edited and annotated by
        C. H. Lange. University of New Mexico Press, Albuquerque.

Hillier, B.
1985   The Nature of the Artificial: The Contingent and the Necessary in
        Spatial Form in Architecture. *Geoforum* 16(2):163–178.
1989   The Architecture of the Urban Object. *Ekistics* 334–335:5–21.
1996   *Space Is the Machine.* Cambridge University Press, Cambridge.

Hillier, B., and J. Hanson
1984   *The Social Logic of Space.* Cambridge University Press, Cambridge.
1987   Introduction: A Second Paradigm. *Architecture and Behaviour*
        3(3):197–199.

Hillier, W., J. Hanson, and H. Graham
1987   Ideas Are in Things: An Application of the Space Syntax Method to
        Discovering House Genotypes. *Environment and Planning B:
        Planning and Design* 14:363–385.

Hillier, B., J. Hanson, and J. Peponis
1987   Syntactic Analysis of Settlements. *Architecture and Behaviour*
        3(3):217–231.

Hillier, B., A. Leaman, P. Stansall, and M. Bedford
1976   Space Syntax. *Environment and Planning B: Planning and Design*
        3:147–185.

Hillier, B., A. Penn, J. Hanson, G. T. Grajewski, and J. Xu
1993   Natural Movement, or, Configuration and Attraction in Urban
        Pedestrian Movement. *Environment and Planning B: Planning and
        Design* 20:29–66.

Hodder, I.
1990   *The Domestication of Europe.* Blackwell, Oxford.

158

1991   *Reading the Past*. Cambridge University Press, Cambridge.

Hopkins, M.
1987   Network Analysis of the Plans of Some Teotihuacan Apartment Compounds. *Environment and Planning B: Planning and Design* 14:387–406.

Horgan, J.
1995   From Complexity to Perplexity. *Scientific American* 272(6):104–109.

Horne, L.
1994   *Village Spaces: Settlement and Society in Northeastern Iran*. Smithsonian Institution Press, Washington, D.C.

Horton, M.
1994   Swahili Architecture, Space and Social Structure. In *Architecture and Order: Approaches to Social Space*, edited by M. P. Pearson and C. Richards, pp. 147–169. Routledge, London.

Howell, T. L.
1996   Identifying Leaders at Hawikku. *Kiva* 62(1):61–82.

Hyslop, J.
1990   *Inka Settlement Planning*. University of Texas Press, Austin.

Iowa, J.
1985   *Ageless Adobe*. Sunstone Press, Santa Fe, New Mexico.

Jackson, J. B.
1954   Pueblo Architecture and Our Own. *Landscape* 3:20–25.

Jeançon, J. A.
1923   *Excavations in the Chama Valley, New Mexico*. Bureau of American Ethnology Bulletin 81. Smithsonian Institution, Washington, D.C.

Johnson, G. A.
1983   Decision-Making Organization and Pastoral Nomad Camp Size. *Human Ecology* 11(2):175–199.
1989   Dynamics of Southwest Prehistory: Far Outside, Looking In. In *Dynamics of Southwest Prehistory*, edited by L. S. Cordell and G. J. Gumerman, pp. 371–389. Smithsonian Institution Press, Washington, D.C.

Judge, W. J.
1973   *The Excavation of Tijeras Pueblo 1971–1973: Preliminary Report, Cibola National Forest, New Mexico*. Report no. 3. USDA Forest Service, Southwest Region, Albuquerque.

Kelley, N. E.
1980   *The Contemporary Ecology of Arroyo Hondo*. School of American Research Press, Santa Fe, New Mexico.

Kent, S.
1990   A Cross-Cultural Study of Segmentation, Architecture, and the Use of Space. In *Domestic Architecture and the Use of Space*, edited by S. Kent, pp. 127–152. Cambridge University Press, Cambridge.

Kidder, A. V.
1958   *Pecos, New Mexico: Archaeological Notes*. Papers of the Robert S. Peabody Foundation for Archaeology, Andover, Massachusetts.

Kroeber, A. L.
1917   *Zuni Kin and Clan*. American Museum of Natural History Reports, vol. 18, part 2, pp. 39–205. New York.

Lambert, M. F.
1954   *Paa-ko: Archaeological Chronicle of an Indian Village in North-Central New Mexico*. Monograph 19, School of American Research, Santa Fe, New Mexico.

Lang, R. W.
1984   Artifacts of Hide, Fur, and Feathers from Arroyo Hondo Pueblo. Additional Report III in *The Faunal Remains from Arroyo Hondo Pueblo, New Mexico: A Study in Short-term Subsistence Change*, by Richard W. Lang and Arthur H. Harris. Arroyo Hondo Archaeological Series, vol. 5. School of American Research Press, Santa Fe, New Mexico.
1986   Artifacts of Woody Materials from Arroyo Hondo Pueblo. Additional Report II in *Food, Diet, and Population at Prehistoric Arroyo Hondo Pueblo, New Mexico*, by W. Wetterstrom. Arroyo Hondo Archaeological Series, vol. 6. School of American Research Press, Santa Fe, New Mexico.
1993   Seriation of Stratigraphic Ceramic Samples from Arroyo Hondo Pueblo. Additional Report I in *The Pottery of Arroyo Hondo Pueblo: Tribalization and Trade in the Northern Rio Grande*, by J. A. Habicht-Mauche. Arroyo Hondo Archaeological Series, vol. 8. School of American Research Press, Santa Fe, New Mexico.

Lang, R. W., and A. H. Harris
1984   *The Faunal Remains from Arroyo Hondo Pueblo, New Mexico: A Study in Short-term Subsistence Change*. Arroyo Hondo Archaeological Series, vol. 5. Santa Fe: School of American Research Press.

Lawrence, D., and S. Low
1990   The Built Environment and Spatial Form. *Annual Review of Anthropology* 19:453–505.

Leach, E.
1978   Does Space Syntax Really Constitute the Social? In *Social Organization and Settlement: Contributions from Anthropology*, pp. 385–401. British Archaeological Reports, International Series, vol. 471. Oxford.

LeBlanc, S. A.
1999   *Prehistoric Warfare in the American Southwest*. University of Utah Press, Salt Lake City.

Ledewitz, S.
1991   Review of *The Social Logic of Space*, by B. Hillier and J. Hanson. *Journal of Architecture and Planning Research* 8(3):260–266.

Lekson, S.H.
1981   Cognitive Frameworks and Chacoan Architecture. *New Mexico Journal of Science* 21(1):27–36.
1988   The Idea of the Kiva in Anasazi Archaeology. *Kiva* 53(3):213–234.
1990   *Mimbres Archaeology of the Upper Gila, New Mexico*. University of Arizona Press, Tucson.

Lekson, S. H., and C. M. Cameron
1995   The Abandonment of Chaco Canyon, the Mesa Verde Migrations, and the Reorganization of the Pueblo World. *Journal of Anthropological Archaeology* 14(2).

Lipe, W.
1995   The Depopulation of the Northern San Juan: Conditions in the Turbulent 1200s. *Journal of Anthropological Archaeology* 14(2):143–169.

Lipton, T.
1992   Tewa Visions of Space: A Study of Settlement Patterns, Architecture, Pottery, and Dance. In *Pueblo Style and Regional Architecture*, edited by N. Markovich, W. F. E. Preiser, and F. Sturm. Van Nostrand Reinhold, New York.

Loo, C.
1977   Beyond the Effects of Crowding: Situational and Individual Differences. In *Perspectives on Environment and Behavior*, edited by D. Stokols, pp. 153–168. Plenum, New York.

161

Low, S.

1995   Indigenous Architecture and the Spanish American Plaza in Mesoamerica and the Caribbean. *American Anthropologist* 97(4):748–762.

Lowell, J. C.

1996   Moieties in Prehistory: A Case Study from the Pueblo Southwest. *Journal of Field Archaeology* 23(1):77–90.

Lycett, M.

1994   Structure and Content in Previous Research: Nels Nelson's Excavations in the Galisteo Basin. Paper presented at the 59th annual meeting of the Society for American Archaeology, Anaheim, California.

Mackey, J.

1980   Arroyo Hondo Population Affinities. Appendix G in *Pueblo Population and Society: The Arroyo Hondo Skeletal and Mortuary Remains*, by A. M. Palkovich. Arroyo Hondo Archaeological Series, vol. 3. School of American Research Press, Santa Fe, New Mexico.

Markus, T. A.

1972   *Building Performance.* John Wiley, New York.

1993   *Buildings and Power.* Routledge, London.

Mazumdar, S., and S. Mazumdar

1994   Societal Values and Architecture: A Socio-Physical Model of the Interrelationships. *Journal of Architecture and Planning Research* 11(1):66–90.

McGuire, R. H., and M. B. Schiffer

1983   A Theory of Architectural Design. *Journal of Anthropological Archaeology* 2:277–303.

Michelson, W.

1970   *Man and His Urban Environment.* Addison-Wesley Press, Reading, Pennsylvania.

Mills, B. J., and P. L. Crown, eds.

1995   *Ceramic Production in the American Southwest.* University of Arizona Press, Tucson.

Mindeleff, V.

1891   *A Study of Pueblo Architecture: Tusayan and Cibola.* Eighth Annual Report of the Bureau of Ethnology to the Secretary of the

Smithsonian Institution, 1886–1887. Government Printing Office, Washington, D.C.

Moholy-Nagy, L.
1995   Space, Space-Time, and the Photographer. In *Poetics of Space: A Critical Photographic Anthology*, edited by S. Yates, pp. 145–156. University of New Mexico Press, Albuquerque.

Moore, J. D.
1992   Pattern and Meaning in Prehistoric Peruvian Architecture: The Architecture of Social Control in the Chimu State. *Latin American Antiquity* 3(2):95–113.
1996   *Architecture and Power in the Ancient Andes.* Cambridge University Press, Cambridge.

Morgan, L. H.
1881   *Houses and House-Life of the American Aborigines.* Contributions to North American Ethnology, vol. 4. Government Printing Office, Washington, D.C.

Morgan, W. N.
1994   *Ancient Architecture of the Southwest.* University of Texas Press, Austin.

Morley, S. G.
1910   *The South House, Puyé.* Bulletin no. 6, Southwest Society. Papers of the School of American Archaeology, old series, no. 7. Santa Fe, New Mexico.

Nabokov, P., and R. Easton
1989   *Native American Architecture.* Oxford University Press, New York.

Nelson, M. C.
1996   Technological Strategies Responsive to Subsistence Stress. In *Evolving Complexity and Environmental Risk in the Prehistoric Southwest,* edited by J. A. Tainter and B. B. Tainter, pp. 107–144. Santa Fe Institute Studies in the Sciences of Complexity, Proceedings vol. 24. Addison-Wesley, Reading, Pennsylvania.

Nelson, N. C.
1914   Arroyo Hondo Pueblo. Unpublished field notes and catalog on file at the Department of Anthropology, American Museum of Natural History, New York.
1915a   Unpublished correspondence regarding Arroyo Hondo Pueblo, New Mexico. American Museum of Natural History, New York.

1915b   Unpublished notes regarding ruins in the Galisteo Basin, New
         Mexico. American Museum of Natural History, New York.

Orcutt, J. D., R. P. Powers, and T. Van Zandt
1994   Big Problems at Big Sites: Interpreting Settlement and
         Demography at Classic and Protohistoric Rio Grande Pueblos.
         Paper presented at the 59th annual meeting of the Society for
         American Archaeology, Anaheim, California.

Orhun, D., B. Hillier, and J. Hanson
1995   Spatial Types in Traditional Turkish Houses. *Environment and
         Planning B: Planning and Design* 22:475–498.

Ortiz, A.
1969   *The Tewa World: Space, Time, Being, and Becoming in a Pueblo Society.*
         University of Chicago Press, Chicago.

Osman, K. M.
1993   Spatial and Aspatial Analysis: A Conceptual Analysis for More
         Informative Design Decisions. Ph.D. dissertation, University of
         Florida, Gainesville.

Osman, K. M., and M. Suliman
1994   The Space Syntax Methodology: Fits and Misfits. *Architecture and
         Behaviour* 10(2):189–204.
1995   Space Syntax: A Modified Algorithm for the Analysis of Non-
         Western Houses. *Open House International* 20(4):46–53.
1996   Spatial and Cultural Dimensions of the Houses of Omdurman,
         Sudan. *Human Relations* 49(4):395–428.

Palkovich, A.
1980   *Pueblo Population and Society: The Arroyo Hondo Skeletal and Mortuary
         Remains.* School of American Research Press, Santa Fe, New
         Mexico.

Pearson, M. P., and C. Richards
1994   Architecture and Order: Spatial Representation and Archaeology.
         In *Architecture and Order: Approaches to Social Space,* edited by
         M. P. Pearson and C. Richards, pp. 38–73. Routledge, London.

Peatross, F. D.
1994   The Spatial Dimensions of Control in Restricted Settings. Ph.D.
         dissertation, Georgia Institute of Technology, Atlanta.

Peckham, S.

1996   The South House at Puyé Reexamined. In *La Jornada: Papers in Honor of William P. Turney*. Papers of the Archaeological Society of New Mexico, no. 22. Albuquerque.

Phagan, C.

1993   The Lithic Artifacts from Arroyo Hondo Pueblo. Part II in *The Pottery from Arroyo Hondo Pueblo: Tribalization and Trade in the Northern Rio Grande*, by J. A. Habicht-Mauche. Arroyo Hondo Archaeological Series, vol. 8. School of American Research, Santa Fe, New Mexico.

Plimpton, C. L., and F. A. Hassan

1987   Social Space: A Determinant of House Architecture. *Environment and Planning B: Planning and Design* 14:439–449.

Prudden, T. M.

1903   The Prehistoric Ruins of the San Juan Watershed in Utah, Arizona, Colorado, and New Mexico. *American Anthropologist* 5(2):224–288.

Ramenofsky, A. F.

1987   *Vectors of Death*. University of New Mexico Press, Albuquerque.

1990   Loss of Innocence: Explanation of Differential Persistence in the Sixteenth-Century Southeast. In *Columbian Consequences*, vol. 2, *Archaeological and Historical Perspectives on the Spanish Borderlands East*, edited by D. H. Thomas, pp. 31–48. Smithsonian Institution Press, Washington, D.C.

Rapoport, A.

1980   Cross-Cultural Aspects of Environmental Design. In *Human Behavior and Environment: Environment and Culture*, vol. 4, edited by I. Altman, A. Rapoport, and J. Wohlwill, pp. 7–46. Plenum, New York.

1990   *History and Precedent in Environmental Design*. Plenum, New York.

Reed, E. K.

1956   Types of Village-Plan Layouts in the Southwest. In *Prehistoric Settlement Patterns in the New World*, edited by G. R. Willey, pp. 11–17. Johnson Reprint, New York.

Reynolds, W. E.

1981   The Ethnoarchaeology of Pueblo Architecture. Ph.D. dissertation, Arizona State University, Tempe.

Richardson, J. B.
1994   *People of the Andes.* St. Remy Press, Montreal.

Roberts, F. H. H.
1935   A Survey of Southwest Archaeology. *American Anthropologist.* 37(1):1–33.

Rohn, A.
1965   Postulation of Socio-economic Groups from Architectural Evidence. *Memoirs of the Society for American Archaeology* 19:65–69.

Roney, J. R.
1996   The Pueblo III Period in the Eastern San Juan and Acoma-Laguna Areas. In *The Prehistoric Pueblo World A.D. 1150–1350*, edited by M. Adler, pp. 145–169. University of Arizona Press, Tucson.

Rose, M. R., J. Dean, and W. Robinson
1981   *The Past Climate of Arroyo Hondo Pueblo, New Mexico, Reconstructed from Tree Rings.* School of American Research Press, Santa Fe, New Mexico.

Saile, D. C.
1977   Architecture in Prehispanic Pueblo Archaeology: Examples from Chaco Canyon, New Mexico. *World Archaeology* 9(2):157–173.
1990   Many Dwellings: Views of a Pueblo World. In *Dwelling, Place, and Environment*, edited by D. Seamon and R. Mugerauer, pp. 159–181. Columbia University Press, New York.

Schaafsma, P., and C. F. Schaafsma
1974   Evidence for the Origin of the Pueblo Kachina Cult as Suggested by Southwestern Rock Art. *American Antiquity* 39:535–545.

Schwartz, D. W.
1971   Background Report on the Archaeology of the Site of Arroyo Hondo: First Arroyo Hondo Field Report. School of American Research, Santa Fe, New Mexico.
1972   Archaeological Investigations at the Arroyo Hondo Site: Second Field Report 1971. School of American Research, Santa Fe, New Mexico.
1981   Population, Culture and Resources: A Rio Grande Pueblo Perspective. In *Geoscience and Man*, vol. XXII.

Schwartz, D. W., and R. W. Lang
1973   Archaeological Investigations at the Arroyo Hondo Site: Third Field

Report 1972. School of American Research, Santa Fe, New Mexico.

Sedgwick, Mrs. W. T.
1926   *Acoma, the Sky City: A Study in Pueblo Indian History and Civilization.* Harvard University Press, Cambridge, Massachusetts.

Service, E.
1962   *Primitive Social Organization.* Random House, New York.

Shafer, H.
1995   Architecture and Symbolism in Transitional Pueblo Development in the Mimbres Valley, SW New Mexico. *Journal of Field Archaeology* 22(1):23–47.

Shapiro, J. S.
1997   Fingerprints on the Landscape: Space Syntax Analysis and Cultural Evolution in the Northern Rio Grande. Ph.D. dissertation, Pennsylvania State University, University Park.
1999   New Light on Old Adobe: A Space Syntax Analysis of the Casa Grande. *Kiva* 64(4):419–446.

Sherrod, D. R., and S. Cohen
1978   Density, Personal Control, and Design. In *Humanscape: Environments for People,* edited by S. Kaplan and R. Kaplan, pp. 331–338. Duxbury Press, North Scituate, Massachusetts.

Simon, H. A.
1962   The Architecture of Complexity. *Proceedings of the American Philosophical Society* 106:467–482.

Smith, M. E.
1983   Pueblo Councils: An Example of Stratified Egalitarianism. In *The Development of Political Organization in Native North America,* edited by E. Tooker, pp. 32–44. American Ethnological Society, New York
1993   Houses and Settlement Hierarchy in Late Postclassic Morelos: A Comparson of Archaeology and Ethnohistory. In *Prehispanic Domestic Units in Western Mesoamerica: Studies of the Household Compound and Residence.* CRC Press, Inc., Boca Raton, LA.

Snead, J.
1996   Political Landscapes, Community Organization, and Mobility along the Rio Sarco. Paper presented at the 61st annual meeting of the Society for American Archaeology, New Orleans.

167

Sommer, F., and S. Aldrich
1995   The Poetic Logic of Art and Aesthetics. In *Poetics of Space: A Critical Photographic Anthology,* edited by S. Yates, pp. 187–196. University of New Mexico Press, Albuquerque.

Spielmann, K.
1994   Clustered Confederacies: Sociopolitical Organization in the Protohistoric Rio Grande. In *The Ancient Southwestern Community,* edited by W. H. Wills and R. D. Leonard, pp. 45–54. University of New Mexico Press, Albuquerque.

Stark, M. T., J. J. Clark, and M. D. Elson
1995   Causes and Consequences of Migration in the Thirteenth-Century Tonto Basin. *Journal of Anthropological Anthropology* 14(2):212–246.

Steadman, S.
1996   Recent Research in the Archaeology of Architecture: Beyond the Foundations. *Journal of Archaeological Research* 4(1):51–93.

Stokols, D.
1976   The Experience of Crowding in Primary and Secondary Environments. *Environment and Behavior* 8(1):49–86.

Stubbs, S.
1950   *Bird's-Eye View of the Pueblos.* University of Oklahoma Press, Norman.

Swentzell, R.
1988   Bupingeh: The Pueblo Plaza. *El Palacio* 94:14–19.
1992   Pueblo Space, Form, and Mythology. In *Pueblo Style and Regional Architecture,* edited by N. Markovich, W. F. E. Preiser, and F. Sturm, pp. 23–30. Van Nostrand Reinhold, New York.

Taaffe, E. J., and H. L. Gauthier
1973   *Geography of Transportation.* Prentice Hall, Englewood Cliffs, New Jersey.

Tainter, J. A., and B. B. Tainter, eds.
1996   *Evolving Complexity and Environmental Risk in the Prehistoric Southwest.* Santa Fe Institute Studies in the Science of Complexity, Proceedings vol. 24. Addison–Wesley, Reading, Pennsylvania.

Thibodeau, Anthony
1993   Miscellaneous Ceramic Artifacts from Arroyo Hondo Pueblo. Additional Report II in *The Pottery of Arroyo Hondo Pueblo:*

168

Tribalization and Trade in the Northern Rio Grande, by J. A. Habicht-Mauche. Arroyo Hondo Archaeological Series, vol. 8. School of American Research Press, Santa Fe, New Mexico.

Trigger, B.
1990   *The Huron: Farmers of the North*. Holt, Rinehart and Winston, Fort Worth, Texas.

United States Department of the Interior, National Park Service
1934   *Old Acoma Pueblo*. Historic American Buildings Survey (Survey no. 36 NM 6). Washington, D.C.

Upham, S.
1982   *Polities and Power*. Academic Press, New York.
1988   East Meets West: Hierarchies and Elites in Pueblo Societies. In *The Sociopolitical Structure of Southwest Societies*, edited by S. Upham and K. Lightfoot, pp. 77–102. Westview Press, Boulder, Colorado.

Venn, T.
1984   Shell Artifacts from Arroyo Hondo Pueblo. Additional Report II in *The Faunal Remains from Arroyo Hondo Pueblo, New Mexico: A Study in Short-term Subsistence Change*, by R. W. Lang and A. H. Harris. Arroyo Hondo Archaeological Series, vol. 5. School of American Research Press, Santa Fe, New Mexico.

Vivian, R. G.
1990   *The Chacoan Prehistory of the San Juan Basin*. Academic Press, San Diego.

Walsh M. R.
1998   Lines in the Sand: Competition and Stone Selection on the Parajito Plateau, New Mexico. *American Antiquity* 63(4):573–593.

Weaver, M. P.
1993   *The Aztecs, Maya, and Their Predecessors: Archaeology of Mesoamerica*. Third edition. Academic Press, Inc., San Diego.

Wetterstrom, W.
1986   *Food, Diet, and Population at Prehistoric Arroyo Hondo Pueblo, New Mexico*. School of American Research Press, Santa Fe, New Mexico.

White, L.
1929   *The Acoma Indians*. Forty-Seventh Annual Report of the Bureau of American Ethnology. Smithsonian Institution, Washington, D.C.

Wilcox, D. R.

1975   A Strategy for Perceiving Social Groups in Puebloan Sites. *Fieldiana Anthropology* 65:120–159.

1996   Pueblo III People and Polity in Relational Context. In *The Prehistoric Pueblo World A.D. 1150–1350*, edited by M. Adler, pp. 241–254. University of Arizona Press, Tucson.

Wilcox, D. R., and J. Haas

1994   The Scream of the Butterfly: Competition and Conflict in the Prehistoric Southwest. In *Themes in Southwestern Prehistory*, edited by G. J. Gumerman, pp. 211–238. School of American Research Press, Santa Fe, New Mexico.

Wilshusen, R.

1989   Architecture as Artifact, Part 2: A Comment on Gilman. *American Antiquity* 54(4):826–833.

Wolpert, J.

1966   Migration as an Adjustment to Environmental Stress. *Journal of Social Issues* 22(4):92–102.

Zedeño, M. N.

1994   A Return to "The Gift": Exploring Prehistoric Reciprocity in the Northern Southwest. Paper presented at the 59th annual meeting of the Society for American Archaeology, Anaheim, California.

Index

abandonment, of Arroyo Hondo, xiii, 30, 31

access analysis: and space syntax analysis of Arroyo Hondo, 60–64; and theoretical foundations of space syntax analysis, 44. *See also* doorways; justified access graphs; rooftops; vents

Acoma Pueblo, 41–42, 43, 108–14, 147n5

Adams, C., 24, 25, 26, 27, 34, 67, 115, 116, 119

aggregation: and architectural changes in northern Rio Grande region in thirteenth century, 23–24; and architectural solutions to need for privacy, 118; and ethnic diversity as factor in social tension in settlements of northern Rio Grande, 115–16. *See also* social organization

agriculture, and economy of Arroyo Hondo, xii, 27. *See also* climate; food shortages; resources

Ahlstrom, R. V. N., 24

alpha index, 43

Altman, I., 117

Anella, T., 64, 70

Ankerl, G., 39

archaeology: and applications of space syntax analysis, 52–58; and background information on Arroyo Hondo, xi–xiv; built environments

and choice of Arroyo Hondo as case study for space syntax analysis, 9–19; connection between architecture and, 4–6, 8. *See also* architecture; ceramics

architecture: and chronology of changes in Rio Grande Valley, 24–26; connection between archaeology and, 4–6, 8; and control issues in northern Southwest, 119–20; and idea of privacy in context of Southwest, 117–18; and innovations as coping mechanisms in periods of social change, 117, 120–21, 124–27; overview of at Arroyo Hondo, 31–38; theoretical background to study of social organization and, 9–16. *See also* doorways; living rooms; plazas; rooftops; space syntax analysis; spatial segregation; storage rooms

Arroyo Hondo Pueblo: Acoma Pueblo compared to, 108–14; approach to space syntax analysis of, xvi–xvii; archaeological background information on, xi–xiv; brief history of, 27–31; choice of as case study for space syntax analysis, 16–19; comparison of other northern Rio Grande settlements to, 94–108; history of research at, ix–xi, 3–4; overview of architecture of, 31–38; publication series on, xiv–xvi; and results of space

171

front-to-back arrangements: and comparison of Puyé Pueblo to Arroyo Hondo, 104, 106; of roomblocks in Component II of Arroyo Hondo, 83, 92, 93

gamma index, 41–42
Gauthier, H. L., 40, 41, 43
Gilman, P., 127
Graham, H., 7
graph theory: and foundations of space syntax analysis, 40, 43–44; potential uses of in anthropology, 15, 53; and topology, 145n1
Greenbie, B. B., 116
Gumerman, G. J., 94

Haas, J., 8, 26, 116, 117
Habicht-Mauche, J. A., xv, 10, 14, 22, 27, 30–31, 34, 70, 92, 93
Hage, P., 15, 53
Hall, E. T., 116, 117, 124
Hanson, J., 6, 7, 9, 34, 40, 44, 45, 47, 48, 51, 52, 54, 56, 57, 70, 145n3
Harary, F., 15, 53
Harris, A. H., xv
Hassan, F. A., 14
Hays-Gilpin, K., 10
Hegmon, M., 118–19
Herr, S., 115, 120, 121
Hewett, E. L., 102
Hieb, L. H., 8
Hill, J., 60
Hillier, B., 6, 7, 9, 34, 40, 44, 45, 47, 48, 51, 52, 54, 56, 57, 70, 145n3
historical documents, and methodology of space syntax analysis, 55
Historic American Buildings Survey (HABS), 41–42, 109, 111
Hodder, I., 11, 116
Hopi, 33, 60, 61, 63
Hopkins, M., 44, 56
Horgan, J., 5
Horne, L., 6, 54
households, and access analysis at Arroyo

Hondo, 60. *See also* living rooms; residence units
Huron, 13

indigenous development model, for population growth in Rio Grande Valley, 22
Inka, 115, 147n6
integration values: and comparison of Acoma Pueblo to Arroyo Hondo, 111, 112–13, 114; and comparison of Puyé Pueblo to Arroyo Hondo, 106; and comparison of Tijeras Pueblo to Arroyo Hondo, 99–101; and computer software, 145–46n3; for kivas at Arroyo Hondo, 119; and methodology of space syntax analysis, 47–49; and social organization of Components I and II of Arroyo Hondo compared, 93; and space syntax analysis of Component I of Arroyo Hondo, 70, 73, 77–78, 86–90, 146n8; and space syntax analysis of Component II of Arroyo Hondo, 83–84, 86–90; and Zuni Pueblo, 58
Iowa, J., 64
Iroquois, 13

Jackson, J. B., 15, 33, 56, 119
Jeançon, J. A., 68, 124
Johnson, G. A., 15, 93, 119
Journal of Anthropological Archaeology (vol. 14, no. 2, 1995), 23
Judge, W. J., 95
justified access graphs: and comparison of Acoma Pueblo to Arroyo Hondo, 111, 112f, 113f; and comparison of Puyé Pueblo to Arroyo Hondo, 105f, 106, 107f, 108f; and comparison of Tijeras Pueblo to Arroyo Hondo, 97–98; and methodology of space syntax analysis, 48–49, 50f, 51t, 52; and space syntax analysis of Component I of Arroyo Hondo, 71f, 74f, 76; and space syntax analysis of